easy
ayurveda
cookbook

easy ayurveda cookbook

30-Minute Recipes to Balance Your Body,
Eat Well, and Still Have Time to Live Your Life

ROCKRIDGE
PRESS

For general information on our other products and services or to obtain technical support, please contact our Customer Care Department within the U.S. at (866) 744-2665, or outside the U.S. at (510) 253-0500.

Rockridge Press publishes its books in a variety of electronic and print formats. Some content that appears in print may not be available in electronic books, and vice versa.

TRADEMARKS: Rockridge Press and the Rockridge Press logo are trademarks or registered trademarks of Callisto Media Inc. and/or its affiliates, in the United States and other countries, and may not be used without written permission. All other trademarks are the property of their respective owners. Rockridge Press is not associated with any product or vendor mentioned in this book.

Photo credits: Fotos mit Geschmack/Stockfood, p. 2; Leigh Beisch/Stockfood, p. 6; Valérie Lhomme/Stockfood, p. 11; Davide Illini/Stocksy, p. 12; Fotos mit Geschmack/Stockfood, p. 16 (top left); Martina Schindler/Stockfood, p. 42; Eising Studio–Food Photo & Video/ Stockfood, p. 54; Canan Czemmel/Stocksy, p. 72; Gemma Comas/ Stockfood, p. 90; Eising Studio–Food Photo & Video/Stockfood, p. 114; Helen Rushbrook/Stocksy, p. 140; Ina Peters/Stocksy, p. 158; Sporrer/Skowronek/Stockfood, p. 172; Ina Peters/Stocksy, p. 188. All other photos Shutterstock.com.

ISBN: Print 978-1-62315-432-5 | eBook 978-1-62315-433-2

QUICK START GUIDE

Inside this book, you'll discover:

- What dosha you are (look for the icons) plus what to eat to bring your health into balance.

- More than 125 recipes designed to be prepared in less than 30 minutes, the time it takes for pizza delivery.

- Dozens of timesaving tips that will shave minutes off your day and give you more time for you.

- Six unique taste profiles, plus how to use them when cooking to better how you look and feel every day.

- Nearly 100 mindfulness tips for staying focused, present, and mindful throughout the day—no matter what life dishes out.

CONTENTS

INTRODUCTION

An Ayurvedic cookbook? You might be asking yourself how
a diet centered on a 5,000-year-old Hindu-based system of
healing can truly benefit your health or fit into your modern
lifestyle. The truth is that the fundamental principles of
Ayurveda are exactly why this book not only works best with
a busy lifestyle but will also help you look and feel better
than ever.

That's a big promise, but Ayurveda delivers because it's not a so-called "diet" created to help you shed pounds or fit into your skinny jeans. It's a traditional medicinal practice designed to nourish your body, mind, and spirit in a gentle, easy way that works no matter how busy or overscheduled your life. In fact, the more hectic your world, the more Ayurveda will work for you. That's because this approach asks you to look at your life holistically, beyond the foods you eat. It takes into account the following aspects of your life:

- ◆ Relationships (are they healthy or toxic?)
- ◆ Workload (do you have work-home balance?)
- ◆ Exercise (are you active or sedentary?)
- ◆ A host of other lifestyle factors that impact your health

Ayurveda works in the modern world because it's based on the notion that you and your lifestyle are unique. One diet won't work the same way for you that it does for someone else. Ayurveda takes these factors into account by helping you identify and understand your predominant *dosha*—one of three energies or collections of physical, mental, and spiritual traits that make up your unique constitution. Furthermore, Ayurveda incorporates ways to determine when your system is out of balance. Because imbalance is the precursor to disease, the practice of Ayurveda can help you regain control over your health.

Finally, food is considered medicine in the practice of Ayurveda. What you eat can serve you or work against you, depending on your dosha as well as your lifestyle at any given moment in time. Foods can make you energetic or lethargic, happy or depressed, strong or weak, and focused or distracted, so what you choose to eat will determine the quality of your health.

This cookbook identifies what foods, activities, and lifestyle factors best serve your particular dosha as well as what specific ingredients you require to put your energy levels back into balance so you can ward off disease, inflammation, and illness. And yes, that in turn can help you lose weight, feel happier, gain energy, and reduce stress.

Inside this book, you'll find more than 125 recipes designed to support the 3 different dosha types; each recipe takes less than 30 minutes to prepare. Handy tips on improving mindfulness, saving time, and incorporating other healthy Ayurvedic principles into your life are also included throughout these pages. You'll take a quiz to determine the characteristics of your personal dosha. Your answers will reveal the associated body type as well as specific foods and activities to incorporate into your life to maximize your health.

Chapters are divided by types of dishes—soups, baked goods, side dishes, main entrées, desserts, beverages, and accompaniments like chutneys and sauces—so you can mix and match foods regardless of time of day. The one exception is breakfast, which has its own chapter.

If you're ready for an eating plan that neatly fits into a busy, hectic life, rather than overhauls it, read on. Guaranteed, you'll soon see why after 5,000 years, this method of healing is still going strong: It works.

1

ANCIENT MEDICINE FOR A MODERN LIFE

Before we dive into the recipes, it helps to understand how Ayurveda started. This will give you a context for the ingredients, preparations, and overall flavors included in each of the dishes. You'll see that Ayurveda is a science, as each recipe and ingredient serves a purpose related to the health and healing of your body. Not only that, but you'll also understand that although this system is based on ancient principles, it's as relevant today in a modern, fast-paced society as it was at its beginning.

Ayurveda's Beginnings

Ayurveda, the world's oldest continuously practiced system of medicinal healing, began more than 5,000 years ago in India. The term *Ayurveda* is Sanskrit and literally translates to *life* ("ayus") *knowledge* ("veda"). While some people associate Ayurveda with spirituality, the truth is that this holistic approach to healing centers on the belief that your health, longevity, and wellness depend on the delicate balance of your mind, body, spirit, and environment. When one of those areas is out of balance in your life, how you look and feel will suffer. Eventually, when imbalance continues long enough, disease, illness, and other health conditions occur, which you experience as symptoms.

The practice is founded on the three doshas:

- ♦ Pitta
- ♦ Vata
- ♦ Kapha

These energies combine to make up your body's mental, emotional, and chemical state, or its *constitution*. Although you will have features of each type of dosha, generally you'll have one that is predominant. To maximize health, happiness, and vitality, Ayurveda recommends identifying which dosha most resembles your basic nature and following diet, exercise, and lifestyle habits that foster that particular way of being.

Any time you experience an interference in your dosha, say a hectic work schedule or a traumatic personal event, Ayurvedic medicine calls on its traditional remedies for healing, including massage, yoga, exercise, herbal remedies, breath or energy work, meditation, diet, and lifestyle changes. While Western medicine would argue that this traditional healing system won't replace modern health advances, Ayurvedic principles make an excellent complement to long-term holistic care.

Why Ayurveda?

Ayurvedic medicine looks at not only your body but also your mind, spirit, and environment, which means you're able to examine your life from a much broader perspective beyond diet or exercise. For instance, do you have a strong work-life balance? How healthy are your relationships? How much time do you spend in nature? Do you nurture your friendships? Are you mindful? Meditative? Enjoying the journey of your life and not just waiting to arrive at a destination to be happy?

Once you determine where your life is out of balance, Ayurveda offers a variety of treatments that are safe, effective, and natural with few to no side effects. A remedy or diagnosis is focused on treating the disease, issue, or imbalance, rather than putting a bandage on your specific symptoms.

Because this healing modality considers food to have healing properties, remedies are natural, such as herbs, foods, and spices. Treatments involve cooking more at home in order to control the quality of ingredients in your diet, or substituting processed foods with whole grains and fresh produce.

Other remedies might include spending more time outdoors to reduce stress, cutting back weekend work hours to create a more balanced home life, or being more mindful to increase energy and happiness. Meditation might be recommended to reduce blood pressure, while reevaluating toxic relationships might be suggested to control anxiety, depression, worry, or fatigue.

Looking at your health through this different kind of lens does more than improve your diet or help you shed pounds; it significantly impacts your quality of life in positive ways.

Ayurveda Today

Ayurveda works synergistically with the modern lifestyle because so much of how we look and feel can be attributed to how we live, not just what we eat.

Because Ayurvedic healing is natural, easy, and holistic, it's designed for people who seek to incorporate healthy practices into their lifestyle, rather than introduce radical and unrealistic changes. Toxins come in a variety of shapes and sizes. This modality helps you identify other areas beyond diet that can create imbalance in your life, such as your environment, relationships, and exercise, and gives you simple strategies for bringing your health back into balance.

That said, diet is one of the easiest places to start adding Ayurvedic health strategies into your routine. Eating is an opportunity to practice mindfulness three to five times a day (a key component of Ayurveda); add spiritual components into your life through gratitude; and enhance your well-being through nutrient-dense ingredients that are based on your own unique constitution.

Adding this practice to your already-hectic schedule might seem daunting, but Ayurveda stresses diet changes, ingredients, recipes, and preparations that are simple to incorporate into a busy life. For instance, recipes in this cookbook are designed to take 30 minutes or less.

Once you start incorporating these principles into your life, you're well positioned to make the switch from curing disease and imbalance to preventing it.

Determine Your Dosha

No two people are alike; therefore, no two treatments will be exactly the same. Knowing and understanding your primary dosha is the first step in Ayurvedic healing. Your dosha refers to your unique, specific collection of personality traits, characteristics, physiological processes, and more, and it falls predominantly into one of these types: vata, kapha, and pitta. Each of these three mind, body, and spirit descriptors have certain tendencies, habits, and ways of being that separate them from the other types. Once you understand your type, as well as your less predominant types, you'll be better able to spot an imbalance and know what to do to put your three doshas back in harmony.

There are three dosha states:

♦ Balanced: All three doshas are in harmony.
♦ Increased: One dosha exists in greater proportion, called "aggravated" or "excess."
♦ Decreased: One dosha exists in lesser proportion, called "depleted" or "reduced."

Typically imbalances occur in your predominant dosha, are most likely experienced in excess, and are usually triggered by stress or diet.

Remedies can include any of the typical Ayurvedic principles, such as massage, yoga, or meditation. This book will focus on diet with mindfulness, lifestyle, and time-saving tips sprinkled throughout to support your ability to get back on track. After all, this practice is all about whole-body healing!

Now, it's time to determine your dosha.

Vata

When associating doshas to natural elements, *vata* personalities mirror the qualities of air and space. That's why their body types tend to be thin, tall, and lanky with prominent joints and bones, while their thoughts and movements are quick, light, and rapidly changing. In the body, vata energy is located in the joints and bones, skin, brain, hair, colon, muscles, nerves, brain, legs, and feet. If vata were an animal, it would be a butterfly—airy with delicate, rapid wings; a thin body; and fast, fluttery actions.

Vata is critical to keep in balance for everyone because it governs the flow or movement of your body: processes like circulation, heartbeat, breathing, blinking, muscle tension, mobility, thoughts, and waste elimination. Without vata, kapha and pitta wouldn't exist, so be sure to keep vata balanced.

Vata in Harmony

When vata is in harmony, you'll experience great creativity, vibrancy, and vitality with heightened senses, enthusiasm, reasoning, memory, and logic. You'll be "in the zone." You'll digest food well and eliminate toxins, like sweat and waste, easily and regularly.

An excitable, joyful, creative personality, this dosha prefers hot weather to cold; warm, nourishing foods to chilled; and tends to crave spice, whether it's in their foods or fragrances, over milder scents and flavors.

Vatas pride themselves in being quick learners who grasp difficult or new concepts and knowledge faster than most, but on the flip side, they'll forget as quickly as they learned. They're fantastic communicators, adept at expressing themselves and typically very social. Often considered the life of the party, they're the ones who are quick to laugh, elevate the mood, and love to have fun. Spontaneous and enthusiastic, they're also the ones who shy away from routine and are happy for last-minute changes in plans. In fact, their moods are just as changeable and impulsive. Because of this, vatas should try to maintain regular habits, routines, and schedules to keep them in balance—mindful and peaceful rather than frenetic, stressed out, and burned out.

Exercise

Vata doshas should enjoy moderately intense activities that keep them engaged without overstimulating them. Frenetic, strenuous, challenging, or competitive workouts can throw them out of balance. Meditative activities like yoga, Pilates, walking, tai chi, qigong, or swimming complement their routines nicely.

Vata Out of Balance

As smart, unpredictable, and energetic as they are, the downside is that they run out of fuel quite easily when they get overly engaged, overexerted, or overworked. In a hectic, busy lifestyle, vatas are quick to become overstimulated and imbalanced, which means they need to use calming techniques to bring their natural constitutions back into balance. They're also quick to become bored, can lack commitment and focus to stay on projects, and seek variety over routine.

If you're vata predominant, you'll know you're out of balance when you have:

- Fear, worry, anxiety, or stress
- Difficulty falling or staying asleep
- A racing mind or distracting thoughts
- Skin problems like dryness, roughness, or breakouts
- Dry or brittle hair
- Pain or issues in the abdomen (digestive or menstrual cramps) or lower back
- Constipation, diarrhea, gas, or bloating
- Fatigue or body aches
- Coughs, sore throat, ear aches, or headaches
- Cold hands and feet

....

TIP *For a quick way to remember what keeps you balanced, think grounding, routine, and warmth.*

....

Restoring Balance Through Foods

When vatas need to get calm, cool, and collected again, they require foods that are heavier, warmer, moister, or oiler— think comfort foods like hot cereals, thick stews, hot milk, roasted vegetables, or nuts—as well as salty, sweet, or sour in flavor. They should avoid foods that are cold, dry, crispy, crunchy, pungent, bitter, or raw as well as cold or raw vegetables and carbonated beverages like seltzers and sodas.

Additional Foods That Support Vata or Pacify an Imbalance

Use these foods when you experience symptoms of imbalance and need to rebalance. You may also rely on them proactively to keep energies in balance if vata is your dosha.

- Chicken or turkey (both organic), wild-caught seafood, or eggs in lieu of red meat or pork for meat eaters.
- Dairy, including yogurt and warm milk (always boil first, according to Ayurvedic principles).
- Grains like rice and wheat, but reduce quantities of rye, oats, buckwheat, and millet.
- Nuts of any type, provided you don't have a nut allergy, especially in warm, spiced recipes.
- Oils of all types pacify, or stabilize, vata.
- Soy (tofu), mung dahl, and other small beans; otherwise reduce intake

of larger gas-producing beans, like black, kidney, red, white, or artisan, gourmet varieties.

♦ Sweeteners of all kinds, including honey, agave, fruit extracts, and sugar, in moderation.

♦ Fruits (warmed, cooked, or eaten alone if possible) that tend to be sour, sweet, or heavy like stone fruits (peaches, avocado, cherries), bananas, tropical fruits (pineapples, mango, papaya), sweet berries, and melons. Limit intake of light, dry, or dried varieties including apples, pears, citrus, cranberries, and pomegranates.

♦ Vegetables (cooked), preferably organic, including asparagus, carrots, and beets. In moderation when cooked with vata-enhancing spices: leafy greens, potatoes, celery, cauliflower, and broccoli. Avoid gas-producing sprouts and cabbage.

♦ Warming spices and herbs (nearly all types), the fresher the better, with the exception of pepper, which should be enjoyed in moderation. Especially supportive are cardamom, ginger, cinnamon, salt, cumin, cloves, and mustard seed.

....

TIP *When vata gets imbalanced and out of sorts, often the easiest way to unwind and relax is to take a 10-minute break to meditate, stretch, breathe, or simply do nothing.*

....

Additional Activities That Support Vata

Beyond diet, there are additional activities you can incorporate into your life to keep vata energies in check. Try these when you feel imbalanced or proactively to support your health before you need to:

♦ Stick to warm temperatures. Keep warm when temperatures drop because vata are prone to colds.

♦ Enjoy warm foods. Limit raw foods or those served chilled.

♦ Indulge in comfort foods that lean toward being warm, heavy, or oily, like stews, casseroles, or roasts.

♦ Maintain regular sleeping hours, including an early bedtime and early wake time.

♦ Incorporate daily self-massage with sesame oil.

♦ Steer clear of stimulants, as the vata personality is prone to excitement.

♦ Keep a daily routine to avoid stress, anxiety, or worry.

♦ Warm spiced milk before bed to encourage sleep.

♦ Change up gym routines to stay engaged and committed to fitness.

♦ Enjoy a variety of hobbies that keep you stimulated mentally.

Kapha

When associating doshas to natural elements, kapha personalities mirror the qualities of earth and water, and in relationship to the pitta and vata energies, kaphas balance them by keeping them grounded. That's why kapha body types tend to be larger, heavier, and more overweight, while their thoughts and movements are slower, more sluggish, and prone to depression. In the body, kapha energy is located in the fatty tissues, throat and lungs, lymph, chest, ligaments, tendons, and connective tissues. If kapha were an animal, it would be a tortoise with its slower, lumbering movements, thicker body, and seemingly thoughtful, deliberate actions.

Kapha in Harmony

When kapha is in harmony, you'll experience enormous feelings of love, joy, happiness, and forgiveness. You'll be easygoing, relaxed, affectionate, and generous while not sweating the small stuff. A calm and peaceful presence, balanced kaphas seem to let life roll right off their backs. Generally speaking, their features lean toward the softer, gentler side as well. With large, inviting eyes; a low, soft voice; and relaxed movements, kaphas come across as quite tranquil, serene, and calm.

This demeanor often puts them in leadership roles or positions of respect in their businesses, communities, and social circles. Even-keeled, good-natured, and dependable, they're the ones you can count on when something needs to get done or a high-pressure situation arises.

Kaphas also pride themselves in being understanding, reliable, stable, loyal, and committed. Unlike vatas, kaphas have big energy that lasts. Physically, they're sturdier, larger, heavier, and more grounded than other doshas with tendencies to be slow moving or sluggish when out of balance. While kaphas aren't as quick thinking as vatas or pittas, they're slower to learn but less likely to forget what they read, hear, or see thanks to an incredible long-term memory.

Exercise

Kapha doshas should enjoy moderately intense aerobic activities that help them resist being sedentary or putting on weight. Unlike vatas, kaphas should engage in strenuous or competitive sports or workouts to keep their fires motivated and stimulated. They're naturals at endurance activities such as basketball, soccer, and marathon running. If they complement their routine with meditative activities, like yoga, Pilates, walking, tai chi, qigong, or swimming, they should choose more strenuous practices and/or ones that push their mental or physical limits. For instance, if they walk, it should be briskly and for 30 minutes or more.

Kapha Out of Balance

Kaphas generally have a relaxed demeanor and the ability to handle stress without missing a beat. In addition, they tend to have very strong immune systems and great health. As even tempered and kind as they tend to be, when out of balance, kaphas can become possessive, overly sensitive, overly attached, addictive, and lazy.

If you're kapha predominant, you'll know you're out of balance when you have:

♦ Insecurity, envy, jealousy, or judgment

♦ Excess weight

♦ Cellulite

♦ Colds, flu, congestion, sinus problems, headaches, and respiratory problems like allergies or asthma

♦ Problems with overeating

♦ Emotional eating habits like late-night snacking, bingeing when stressed, and eating sugary foods to soothe negative feelings

♦ Little to no exercise in your daily routine; laziness

♦ Bad TV habits, like weekend TV marathons or days spent on the couch watching reruns

♦ No desire for intellectual or physical stimulation

♦ Difficulty making or committing to social engagements

♦ Homebody tendencies

♦ Feelings of possessiveness or materialism

♦ Resistance to change

♦ Toxic or difficult relationships, often where you're getting the short end of the stick

♦ Dry skin or hair (Kaphas are known for silky, hydrated, healthy skin and hair.)

♦ A dull, lifeless outlook on life

♦ Oversensitivity

♦ Addictions

♦ Excessive sleep or napping

Restoring Balance Through Foods

When kaphas need inspiration, excitement, and motivation, they should opt for dry, spicy, warming, or light foods that perk them up and give them a boost of energy. Think spiced teas, zesty citrus, or foods with ginger, garlic, or pepper. They should avoid heavy, sour, cold, sweet, or watery foods.

Additional Foods That Support Kapha

Use these foods when you experience symptoms of imbalance and need to rebalance, or proactively to keep energies in balance if this is your body type:

♦ Barley, millet, buckwheat, and rye over oats, rice, and wheat.

- Beans of all types—large and small—with the exception of soybeans (tofu).

- Ginger tea to stimulate slow digestion.

- Oils in very limited quantities, and stick to olive oil, ghee, almond oil, or mustard oil.

- Seeds and nuts on a limited basis, although pumpkin and sunflower seeds can be enjoyed in moderation.

- Spices of all types, especially invigorating ones like ginger, black pepper, chilies, cumin, or cinnamon, while avoiding salt.

- Vegetables of all types, preferably organic, with the exception of those that are starchier, moister, and more sugary, like sweet potatoes, zucchini, squash, corn, and tomatoes.

- Dark, bitter greens like endive.

- Lighter, smaller meals eaten frequently, with your largest meal at lunchtime and the smallest at dinner—and no meals within three hours of sleep.

- Lighter fruits like apples, pears, cranberries, pomegranates, and apricots instead of heavier options like tropical fruits, stone fruits, bananas, melons, dates, and figs.

- More raw foods than cooked.

....

TIP *For a quick way to remember what keeps you balanced, think stimulation, self-expression, and dryness.*

....

- Pungent, bitter, and astringent foods, while avoiding sugary, oily, or buttery options.

- Raw honey in limited amounts, but avoid other sweeteners.

- Stimulating, hot, or spicy flavors, ingredients, or cuisines.

- Warm coffees, teas, or meals, while avoiding cold foods or drinks.

- Zesty citrus flavors like lemon or lime.

Additional Activities That Support Kapha

Beyond diet, there are additional activities you can incorporate into your life to keep kapha energies in check. Try these when you feel imbalanced, or be proactive to support your good health:

- Any routines or regimens that are new or different, including something as simple as a new route to work, a different gym class, or a change in hobbies.

- Social events that require you to socialize and meet new people.

- Experiences that stretch your mind, body, or spirit to think, feel, move, or engage in a different way.

- Stimulating activities that require quick thinking or frenetic movements.

- Avoid sugary, oily, or processed foods.

- Avoid too much relaxation, indulgence, or leisure.

- Maintain a regular sleep routine—early to bed and early to rise—with no naps during the day.

- Create personal boundaries to prevent your nice nature from being taken advantage of.

- Spend time in warm climates or environments, like saunas or beaches.

- Use rejuvenating aromatherapy scents (eucalyptus, for example) to invigorate or energize you throughout the day.

- Walk, bike, or stretch after meals to keep moving and avoid lethargy.

- Distract yourself from eating when you're feeling emotional by phoning a friend, taking a walk, or engaging in an activity you love.

- Incorporate a dry self-massage (i.e., using no oils or lotions) morning and night to increase circulation and energy levels.

- Add workouts that are challenging, uplifting, frenetic, or competitive, like dancing, running, kickboxing, cycling, or aerobics.

- Trade out neutral or muted fashions for fabrics with bright colors or interesting patterns.

Pitta

When associating doshas to natural elements, pitta personalities mirror the qualities of fire and water. Pittas balance vata and kapha energies by keeping them fired up. The pitta dosha is associated with transformation and change, so they're generally considered more flexible and nimble, both in body type and thinking. Pittas are also able to move quickly into action. Pitta body types tend to have a medium build with strong muscle development, warm or oily skin, and loads of body heat. Their thoughts and actions are passionate, expressive, loud, strong, and prone to dominating conversations.

In the body, pitta energy is located in the stomach, liver, spleen, small intestine, blood, eyes, sweat, and pancreas. By nature, they tend to overheat both physically and mentally when under stress. If pitta were an animal, they'd be a tiger because of the hot, sharp, aggressive, fluid, acidic, and acerbic qualities demonstrated in their physical and mental acuity.

Pitta in Harmony

When pitta is in harmony, you'll experience contentment, confidence, focus, strength, and intelligence. Pittas tend to have strong impulses and desires, including a healthy appetite for food, sex, and social interaction. They're highly extroverted, intelligent, and insightful and often steer the attention and spotlight to themselves—a situation they love. And people love to be around the pitta energy because it's joyful, radiant, powerful, courageous, and mentally astute.

Pittas also pride themselves in being focused, decisive, successful, ambitious, and highly competitive. You'll often find them at sporting events, either participating or playing, and striving to be the best at whatever they endeavor to do. Because they're so willful and energetic, pittas achieve what they set out to do and get what they want out of life.

This demeanor often finds them in leadership roles in business, politics, or social networks where their public speaking prowess, managerial skills, and entrepreneurial abilities can be on full display.

Exercise

Pitta doshas are very self-motivating and need no incentive to push themselves to participate in strenuous or competitive sports or workouts. Their challenge is to not become overly competitive, serious, or hard on themselves. Instead, they should remember to have fun and enjoy their activities, versus being the best or pushing themselves to win no matter what it takes. Pittas should complement their routine with leisurely or meditative activities, like yoga, Pilates, walking, tai chi, qigong, or swimming. Pittas love a pool. They can swim off pent-up aggression and cool off their innate fire.

Pitta Out of Balance

If you're pitta predominant, you'll know you're out of balance when you have:

♦ Ulcers or other symptoms of repressed feelings

♦ Anger, rage, irritability, or judgmental thoughts

♦ Temper tantrums or outbursts

♦ Impatience with others, both at home and work

♦ Skin problems like rashes, eczema, bruises, sunburn, boils, skin cancer, freckles, or acne

♦ Gray, thinning hair or baldness

♦ Overly controlling nature about money

♦ Overly narcissistic or attention-seeking tendencies

♦ Addictions like caffeine, nicotine, or alcohol, which are stimulants that quickly put their energies out of whack

♦ A competitive streak on overdrive

♦ Mood swings that quickly move from laughter to arguments

♦ Excess sweat or overheating

♦ Bitterness about your life

♦ Harsh, overbearing opinions about others

♦ Inflammation in the body that results in fever, disease, or infection

♦ Digestive issues like heartburn or acid stomach

♦ Insomnia or fatigue

♦ Extreme perfectionism

Restoring Balance Through Foods

Pittas need cooling, calming foods to balance their fiery demeanor; therefore, they should eat more cool, juicy, and sweet foods, rather than sour, spicy, salty, oily, acidic, or warm options.

Additional Foods That Support Pitta

Use these foods when you experience symptoms of imbalance and need to rebalance. You may also rely on them proactively to keep energies in balance if pitta is your dosha:

♦ Apples, mango, melons, grapes, lychee, dates, coconut, and pomegranate, but avoid apricots, berries, cherries, citrus, tropical fruits, plums, and rhubarb.

♦ Beans of any type are fantastic, with the exception of lentils.

♦ Bell peppers, Brussels sprouts, cucumber, cauliflower, broccoli, asparagus, celery, lettuce, peas, mushrooms, potatoes, squash, zucchini, celery, corn, and parsnip. Limit beets, carrots, chilies, pickled veggies, radish, spinach, turnip, toma-toes, carrots, avocados, and eggplant.

- Butter (unsalted), buttermilk, soft cheese, sweet lassi, and ghee, but limit heavier or sour dairy products like yogurt, ice cream, sour butter-milk, hard cheese, and sour cream.

- Grains like barley, rice, oats, and wheat, but not millet, buckwheat, rye, or corn.

- Herbs and spices like turmeric, lemon-grass, mint, rose, cardamom, cori-ander, dill, fennel, and cumin, which have cooling, calming properties. Limit heat generators like basil, bay leaves, caraway, cinnamon, mustard seed, onion, cayenne, sage, garlic, ginger, nutmeg, or chilies.

- Salads and leafy greens like kale, arugula, dandelions, and endive.

- Sunflower, soy, and coconut oils work well with this body type. Use corn, sesame, peanut, almond, and olive oils in moderation.

- Sunflower and pumpkin seeds and coconut are suggested, but reduce intake of all other nuts and sesame seeds.

- Cool drinks like fruit and vegetables juices, chilled water or milk, and coconut milk are ideal. Limit coffee, tea, and other hot drinks, plus alcohol and carbonated drinks like seltzer and sodas.

- Natural sweeteners like sugar, honey, agave or fruit nectars, rather than artificial sweeteners.

Additional Activities That Support Pitta

Beyond diet, there are additional activi-ties you can incorporate into your life to keep pitta energies in check. Try these when you feel imbalanced; rely on them proactively to support good health:

- Spend time in nature.

- Enjoy friends and family in relaxed environments, such as during a walk after dinner or taking a yoga class together.

- Physical exercise that is calming and doesn't lend itself to overheating or competitiveness, like swimming, tai chi, qigong, walking, yoga, or stretching.

- Regular mealtimes. (Pittas don't like to skip meals.)

- Short work breaks throughout the day to stay mindful, focus on breath, or meditate.

- Cool or moist environments rather than hot weather, sun, or heat, which makes pittas tired and overheated.

- Avoid cigarettes and alcohol.

- To calm you when you're feeling stressed, try 1 teaspoon of rose petal jam on crackers, toast, or plain.

- Avoid overworking, and instead com-mit to work-life balance.

....

TIP *For a quick way to remember what keeps you balanced, think calm, moder-ation, and cooling.*
....

- Limit fried, pickled, and spicy foods, which contribute to pittas' overheating.
- Charity or other nonprofit work that cultivates generosity, sharing, patience, honesty, kindness, and ethics over achievement, competition, and aggression.
- Meditation.
- Anger management exercises or therapy.
- Self-massage five minutes a day with coconut oil anywhere there's tension, especially feet and scalp.
- Start the day with ½ cup aloe vera juice combined with ½ cup pomegranate or apple juice instead of coffee or black tea.
- A cool bath or shower before bedtime to help you sleep.
- Cool evening walks when the sun goes down to relax you after a tough day.
- No electronics or exercise after work to allow time to relax before bed.
- Lunches that contain cooling foods, as pitta dosha energy peaks between 10 a.m. and 2 p.m., causing you to crave the wrong foods like onions, garlic, chilies, and other warming spices and herbs.

Finding You

Take this quiz to determine your predominant dosha energy. If two answers apply, choose the one that resembles you most of the time. Tally your responses at the bottom of the quiz.

1. My body type can be best described as:
a. Thin, slender with lean muscles
b. Medium build with good muscle tone
c. Large or stocky frame with little muscle tone

2. Which describes your weight maintenance?
a. I lose weight easily and have trouble gaining
b. I maintain even weight, plus or minus a few pounds
c. I gain weight easily and have trouble losing

3. My skin type can best be described as:
a. Thin, dry, or rough
b. Warm, reddish, and sensitive
c. Oily, hydrated, and thick

4. I find routine to be:
a. Challenging
b. Somewhat challenging
c. Quite comfortable

5. When it comes to planning activities:
a. I don't need to plan; I'm active
b. I have a plan and complete it
c. I'm happy if someone else does the planning

6. When I speak:
a. I'm fast and have a lot to say
b. I'm direct, to the point, and assertive
c. I listen more than I speak

7. I sleep:
a. Minimal amounts, four to six hours, most of it restless with difficulty falling asleep
b. Six to seven hours, waking sometimes but easily going back to sleep
c. Deeply for eight or more hours and like naps during the day

8. When stressed, my demeanor tends to be:
a. Anxious or worried
b. Impatient or irritable
c. Calm, cool, and even

9. My body temperature runs:
a. Cold—my hands and feet are cold, and I prefer warm surroundings
b. Warm regardless of season or geography, so I prefer cooler surroundings
c. Neutrally—I adapt to temperatures but dislike cold, rainy, or damp days

10. The weather I like the least:
a. Cold
b. Hot
c. Wet or damp

11. My appetite is:
a. Variable: I eat quickly and have delicate or temperamental digestion *A*
b. Voracious: I love to eat and can handle any foods *T*
c. Sporadic: I eat slowly and can skip meals with no problem

12. My thirst is:
a. Variable: Sometimes I'm thirsty, while other times I'm not *A*
b. Insatiable: I drink a lot of water *T*
c. Low, and I don't feel thirsty often

13. When it comes to spending money:
a. I'm impulsive and frivolous *A*
b. I'll invest in luxury items *T*
c. I'm a saver, not a spender

14. Decision-making:
a. is difficult for me, as I'm indecisive *T*
b. is easy for me, as I'm purposeful, driven, and methodic *A*
c. is not my thing, as I'm happier if someone else makes the choices

15. My taste preferences lean toward:
a. Salty *T*
b. Sour
c. Sweet *A*

16. My activity levels can be described as:
a. Active: I'm constantly on the go *T*
b. Purposeful: I prefer competitive physical activities
c. Leisurely: I like low-stress, low-effort recreation *A*

17. My stamina levels can be described as:
a. Touch and go: I get worn out quickly
b. Strong: I'm able to perform a variety of physical activities *T A*
c. Great: I have fantastic endurance

18. My moods change:
a. Rapidly *T*
b. Slowly *A*
c. Steadily, if at all

19. When forming opinions:
a. I generate ideas and can change my mind on a whim *T*
b. I find facts before making up my mind *A*
c. I make up my mind quickly, then don't change it

20. My attention span is:
a. Short *T*
b. Long, and I focus on details
c. Long, and I focus on the big picture *A*

....

Mostly As are vata.
Mostly Bs are pitta.
Mostly Cs are kapha.
....

What Are Blended Doshas?

Most people have one dominant dosha, but in some instances, you might have two equal doshas—called "double," "dual," or blended doshas—with a third lesser energy. For example, you might be vata-pitta dominant in terms of your personality and exercise habits, but with the occasional kapha trait or tendency. Say you have long-lasting, deep friendships. If you've got double doshas, those energies don't necessarily "blend." In other words, if you're vata-pitta, you won't have one big compilation of vata and pitta tendencies running all the time. Instead, you'll find that one dosha is more prominent than the other, depending on the day, the situation, your environment, or certain circumstances going on in your life.

Conversely, you can also be one dosha in your mind and another in your body. For example, you can have vata physical characteristics—tall, lanky, and energetic with frenetic motions—but a kapha mindset in how you approach aspects of your life. Say you're more relaxed or confident about work, rather than worried, or you're more cool and quiet in social situations, rather than the life of the party.

Double Doshas

The three types of double doshas are:

- ♦ Vata-pitta
- ♦ Pitta-kapha
- ♦ Kapha-vata

Vata-Pitta

Read about both vata and pitta doshas to determine which traits resonate most with you. If you're vata in the body, then your physique likely follows that of a typical vata-dominant energy: You're thin, energetic, and mobile as well as a great conversationalist who is energetic, spontaneous, and fun loving. Pitta mental traits will add a touch of fire, even irritability, along with better digestion and circulation.

Pitta energies in the body will give you a more medium build with greater muscle tone, complemented by the vata mental energies that pull you toward anxiety, stress, and worry.

Because vata and pitta have drying characteristics, you need to focus on a diet that contains moist, oily, and hydrating foods to keep skin, hair, joints, and tissues lubricated. Minimize light, dry, or hot foods while incorporating sweeter options. Salty, pungent, and bitter flavors should be avoided.

Vata-pitta energies can stay in harmony better by the seasons: pacifying or stabilizing pitta in the hot weather, while reducing vata in the cooler fall and winter months.

Pitta-Kapha

Read about both pitta and kapha doshas to determine which traits resonate most with you. If kapha dosha is dominant in the body, you'll likely have a sturdier, stockier frame, with some muscle tone thanks to pitta characteristics. Mentally, you'll be more ambitious, competitive, driven, and social thanks to pitta energy, and at times, even quicker to anger, judgment, or impatience.

If pitta is present in the body, look for a more medium build with good muscle tone and a more laid-back, easygoing way of being. On the downside, kapha energies can have a tendency to make the normally work-hard, play-hard pittas lazier and less motivated than they'd normally be.

Because both energies share the water elements, this double dosha should focus on foods that are astringent and drying, rather than oily, sweet, or moist.

Pitta-kapha energies can stay in harmony better by the seasons: pacifying pitta in the hot weather, while reducing kapha in the cold, damp winter and spring months.

Kapha-Vata

Read about both vata and kapha doshas to determine which traits resonate most with you. That said, this combination isn't often seen because these two energies tend to be direct opposites in many ways. Think about the energetic and mobile nature of the butterfly-like vata energy combined with the slower, more sedentary tortoise-like kapha nature.

If you're vata-predominant in the body, you'll likely have the thinner frame combined with the chilled-out, peaceful demeanor of the kapha energy.

However, a kapha-predominant body type lends itself to a larger frame with potential for weight gain, combined with the more energetic, creative, and enthusiastic love of life from the vata dosha.

In terms of diet, kapha-vatas should seek warm foods because fire is a missing element in their constitution, and they're often imbalanced by cold foods, cold weather, over- or under-eating, and fasting. Because the vata energy causes you to eat fast while kapha tends toward emotional eating, you'll find this dual dosha tends to rely on convenience foods, like empty-calorie junk foods.

How to Bring Your Dosha into Balance

The health of your mind, body, and spirit becomes compromised when any of the doshas become imbalanced, i.e., excessive or aggravated, which is why it's critical to keep them in check. These imbalances usually occur because of a number of lifestyle factors, ranging from your environment to your relationships to your diet and exercise regimen.

The first step in bringing your dosha into balance is identifying your dosha type. Learn to recognize typical causes and symptoms of imbalance for your dosha. That way, when life becomes overwhelming, you're quick to spot the issues and start the remedies that will work for your dosha type.

Warm Up Vata Imbalances

Excess stress usually throws the vata energy out of whack, making you feel out of control, worried, anxious, and restless. You may skip meals and start to lose

Hot Versus Cold Foods   *In Ayurveda, foods, drinks, spices, and herbs are deemed either hot or cold, meaning that they create heat in your body when you consume them or cooling effects. This can refer to temperature—for example, cold drinks like smoothies are cooling while hot drinks like coffee are warming—or it can refer to the effects they produce in your body. Cayenne, for instance, is spicy and stimulating and therefore dials up the heat in your body. The flavor, scent, and other properties of mint, on the other hand, inherently cool your body. These properties can be used to naturally balance the energies in your body. Say you're a pitta who tends to run hot; you'll want naturally cooling foods when out of balance.*

weight. To bring this dosha back into balance, it's critical to pacify (or stabilize) through foods that mitigate the excess. Because vata energy is naturally light, dry, airy, and cool (think about the airy butterfly), choose foods that are heavier, oilier, denser, and warmer to achieve harmony. While vatas naturally gravitate toward pungent, bitter, and astringent foods, those are the ones you should avoid if imbalanced. Instead, opt for sweet, salty, or sour foods to pacify your system and keep it grounded, uplifted, and confident.

Cool Down Pitta Imbalances

Pitta imbalances are often visible first in the skin with inflammation, redness, itchy patches, or hot flushes, or with inflammatory physical and mental issues like infection, fever, anger, or ulcers. To bring this dosha back into balance, it's critical to pacify (or stabilize) through foods that mitigate the excess fire. Because pitta energy is naturally hot and intense (think about the fiery tiger), choose foods that are cooler, lighter, fresher, and more refreshing to achieve harmony. While pittas naturally gravitate toward spicy, salty, pungent, or sour options that increase heat and inflammation, those are the ones you should avoid if imbalanced. Instead, opt for sweet, bitter, or astringent foods to pacify your system and keep you cool and calm. Avoid coffee, tea, chocolate, yogurt, animal products, and alcohol.

Even Out Kapha Imbalances

Kapha energies naturally increase during cold-weather months, which impacts how we eat, how much activity we get, and our mood, which contributes to colds, flu, and increased phlegm. To bring kapha back into balance, it's critical to pacify (or stabilize) through foods that mitigate the excess sluggishness or apathy. Because kapha energy is naturally slow, calm, and sensitive (think about the peaceful tortoise), choose foods that are hotter, lighter, drier, and more stimulating to achieve harmony. While kaphas naturally gravitate toward sweet, salty, or sour options, those are the ones you should avoid if imbalanced. Instead, opt for pungent, bitter, or astringent foods to pacify your system, including heating spices like peppers, ginger, cinnamon, cumin, and chilies or light, dry, and warm foods. Avoid cool meals or drinks, junk foods, carbonated drinks, red meat, or highly processed options.

Understanding the Food Groups

Ayurveda breaks up food, medicine, and people into three *gunas*:

♦ Tamasic

♦ Rajasic

♦ Sattvic

They are associated with a dominant nature, specific characteristics, and unique qualities. These gunas are sometimes referred to as *mind doshas*. While you have all three gunas present in your personality and ways of being, one can become more dominant than the other depending on diet, lifestyle, circumstances, and more.

Tamasic

Tamasic characteristics tend to be laziness, insensitivity, ignorance, or deceit. This includes dry, distasteful, unpalatable, or tainted foods, such as those that are highly processed, canned, outdated, frozen, or incompatible (e.g., fish and dairy). Alcohol, red meat, eggs, and fish fall into this category.

Tamasic foods are said to be the basis of lowered consciousness—doubt, ignorance, negativity, and pessimism.

Rajasic

Rajasic characteristics tend to be materialism, a focus on instant or sensory indulgence, greed, passion, and spontaneity. This category includes salty, pungent, hot, dry, sour, and bitter foods, such as deep-fried vegetables or stimulating spices. Overeating also increases raja.

Rajasic foods are said to be the basis of movement, motion, pain, and energy.

Sattvic

Sattvic characteristics tend to be gentleness, sensitivity, patience, kindness, and tolerance. This includes juicy, sweet, light, flavorful, and energy-producing foods like fresh fruits and vegetables, herbs, beans, spices, grains, nuts, and compatible foods.

Because the mind and body are so intricately linked, focusing on or increasing consumption of certain guna activities or foods over another can create imbalances in the mind that lead to excesses in the body. Later those imbalances can cause disease or other health issues. Similarly, imbalances in your dosha can impact your mind.

To maximize health in today's modern world, your goal is to eat as many sattvic foods as possible to increase that guna, supplemented with rajasic foods. Tamasic foods should be avoided as much as possible. Sattvic foods are said to be the basis of elevated consciousness.

Understanding the Six Tastes

The Ayurvedic diet includes six distinct tastes that energetically impact your mind and body, depending on your dosha type:

- Astringent
- Bitter
- Pungent
- Salty
- Sour
- Sweet

Each taste either aggravates a particular dosha or pacifies it. One of the Ayurvedic principles says: "Like energies create like energies." Therefore, if you've got an excess of a certain type of energy, say, the fiery pitta, then you'll aggravate or increase that excess by adding pungent, sour, salty, or other heat-inducing flavors and ingredients. Conversely, sweet, bitter, or astringent tastes decrease excess pitta energy and bring your system back into balance.

Ayurveda recommends eating all six tastes at every meal to ensure that not only is your dosha energy balanced and satisfied, but you're also maximizing vitamins, nutrients, and minerals from a well-rounded diet. You'll see this principle in Indian cooking, with its variety of spices, pastes, and chutneys present at every dinner. Remember that most foods, spices, and herbs contain more than one taste. For instance, turmeric can be astringent, bitter, and sweet; oranges are sour and sweet; and apples can be astringent and sweet.

Balancing the Tastes
Vata = sweet, sour, salty
Pitta = sweet, bitter, astringent
Kapha = pungent, bitter, astringent

Guidelines and Food Sources

For a fully balanced meal, try to incorporate as many of the six tastes as possible. Add more or less of a particular taste depending on your dosha and/or imbalances.

Astringent

Use this to balance kapha and pitta because it reduces inflammation. Too much can throw vata out of whack. Astringent foods include asparagus, lentils, cauliflower, pomegranates, grapes, green apples, and beans because of their tannins.

Bitter

Use this to balance kapha and pitta because it detoxifies your organs, cells, and systems. Too much can throw vata energies out of sorts and cause digestive distress. Bitter foods include broccoli, beets, celery, sprouts, leafy greens like kale, and green and yellow vegetables because of their alkaloid or glycoside content.

Pungent

Use this to balance kapha because it stimulates sweat glands and clears your sinuses. Too much can throw pitta and vata energies out of sorts. Pungent foods include cayenne, cloves, black pepper, ginger, chilies, mustard, onions, and garlic because of their essential oils.

Salty

Use this to balance vata because it stimulates your appetite and enhances flavors in your foods. Too much can throw pitta and kapha energies out of sorts. Salty foods include soy sauce, fish, fish sauce, salt, and salted or cured meats because of their high quantity of mineral salts.

Sour

Use this to balance vata because it stimulates your appetite and eases digestion. Too much can throw pitta and kapha energies out of sorts. Sour foods include pickled options, vinegars, tomatoes, alcohol, salad dressings, citrus, and berries because of their natural acidity.

Sweet

Use this to balance vata and pitta because of its soothing, satisfying effect on your body and emotions. Watch how much you consume, or focus primarily on whole fruits, because too much leads to weight gain and can exacerbate the kapha dosha. Sweet foods include honey, rice, bread, grains, pasta, chicken, meat, dairy, sugar, and molasses because of their fat, protein, and carbohydrate contents.

2

BEVERAGES

CARDAMOM-MINT WATER

PREP TIME: 5 MINUTES / COOK TIME: 5 TO 10 MINUTES

VATA

1

SERVING

SEASONS: FALL/WINTER

TASTES: PUNGENT, SWEET

Vatas *can add cinnamon sticks for more digestive aid.*

Pittas *can add more fennel and mint to aid in cooling. Drink at room temperature or slightly chilled, not hot.*

Kaphas *can add ginger or lemon zest for more uplifting flavor.*

Cardamom is considered tridoshic, which means it's great for balancing all dosha types. Feel free to adjust this recipe by adding spices that support your particular dosha. Prepare and sip throughout the day.

8 cups water
1 handful mint
½ cup fennel seeds
½ cup cardamom seeds

1. In a large pot, boil the water.

2. Add the mint, fennel seeds, and cardamom seeds, and turn off the heat.

3. Steep as the water cools.

4. Enjoy at room temperature.

> **Tip:** *Strain off the spices for lighter flavor or leave in as you sip throughout the day for stronger flavor.*

CLOVE–FENNEL ROSEWATER

PREP TIME: 5 MINUTES / COOK TIME: 5 TO 10 MINUTES

Cloves, fennel, and rose petals are excellent for cooling the fiery properties of the pitta dosha. The sweet rose petal and spicy red clove scents swirl together to create an intoxicating aroma. Prepare and sip throughout the day.

8 cups water

1 handful rose petals

½ cup fennel seeds

¼ cup red cloves

1. In a medium pot, boil the water.

2. Add the rose petals, fennel seeds, and red cloves, and turn off the heat.

3. Steep as the water cools.

4. Enjoy at room temperature.

PITTA

1

SERVING

SEASONS: ALL SEASONS, ESPECIALLY SUMMER

TASTES: BITTER, SWEET, ASTRINGENT

Vatas *can substitute mint and cinnamon sticks for more digestive aid and add honey.*

Pittas *can add more of any of the spices to aid in cooling. Be sure to drink at room temperature or slightly chilled, not hot.*

Kaphas *can add ginger or lemon zest for more uplifting flavor and honey to sweeten.*

Mindfulness Tip: *Activate all your senses when you eat. Notice the bright, vibrant colors in your salad, inhale the aromas of the different foods on your plate, listen to the crunch as you cut into a crispy vegetable, feel the textures of ingredients as you chew, and notice the different flavors on your tongue.*

GINGER–BASIL FIZZY WATER

PREP TIME: 5 MINUTES

KAPHA

1

SERVING

SEASONS: ALL SEASONS,
ESPECIALLY SPRING

TASTES: ASTRINGENT,
PUNGENT, SOUR, SWEET

Vatas *can garnish with mint for more support and use still water, rather than sparkling.*

Pittas *should halve the amount of ginger and honey, garnish with mint, and alternate between sparkling water and flat.*

Kaphas *can add ginger or lemon zest for more uplifting flavor.*

Lemon, ginger, and basil are great for rejuvenating and uplifting the mind, body, and spirit, particularly when paired with an effervescent sparkling water. Ginger-Basil Fizzy Water also makes a refreshing alternative to sugar-packed lemon-lime soda or ginger ale.

1 (2-inch) ginger knob, peeled
Juice of 1 lemon
⅛ to ¼ cup raw honey, depending on your tastes
8 cups sparkling water (can use flavored)
Fresh basil sprigs, for garnish

1. In a blender, blend the ginger, lemon juice, and honey until well combined.

2. Pour a few tablespoons of the mixture into a glass, then fill the glass with the sparkling water.

3. Add more mixture to taste, garnish with the basil, and enjoy.

Ayurvedic Lifestyle Tip: *Avoid eating fish with milk or yogurt, which creates toxins in the body, according to Ayurvedic principles.*

SAFFRON–LEMON SWEET TEA

PREP TIME: 3 MINUTES / COOK TIME: 10 MINUTES

This is a nice twist on the warm lemon water many detoxes or cleanses advise as a way to start your day. Extra spices give this tea more depth and provide additional dosha balance.

5 cups water

1 tablespoon cardamom seeds

¼ teaspoon saffron

1 tablespoon fennel seeds

Zest of 1 lemon

1 tablespoon raw honey

1. In a medium pot, boil the water, cardamom seeds, saffron, fennel seeds, and lemon zest for 5 minutes.

2. Remove from the heat and let stand for another 5 minutes.

3. Stir in the honey and serve.

VATA

2–4
SERVINGS

SEASONS: AUTUMN/WINTER

TASTES: ASTRINGENT, PUNGENT, SOUR, SWEET

Vatas *can add more of any of the spices for more support.*

Pittas *should halve or omit the honey. Fresh lemon should be used sparingly, so consider halving the zest.*

Kaphas *can add ginger for more uplifting flavor and go lighter on the honey.*

Timesaving Tip: *Invest in a label maker and use it to mark storage boxes, in-cabinet trays, and shelving bins. Next time you're hunting for a bandage, extension cord, or rarely used kitchen gadget, you'll know exactly where to look.*

CUMIN–CILANTRO TEA WITH ROSE PETALS

PREP TIME: 3 MINUTES / COOK TIME: 10 MINUTES

PITTA

2–4
SERVINGS

SEASON: SUMMER

TASTES: ASTRINGENT, BITTER, PUNGENT, SOUR, SWEET

Vatas *can add more of any of the spices for more support.*

Pittas *can increase any of the ingredients as desired.*

Kaphas *can omit the rose petals and add ginger and cloves for more uplifting flavor and honey for sweetness.*

Pitta doshas will love the calming nature of this flavorful tea. While the spices below are tridoshic, you can vary the recipe by adding spices and herbs that target your particular energies.

5 cups water

3 tablespoons cumin seeds

3 or 4 rose petals

¼ cup fresh cilantro leaves

1. In a medium pot, boil the water, cumin seeds, rose petals, and cilantro for 5 minutes.

2. Remove from the heat and let stand for another 5 minutes.

3. Strain the tea into cups and serve.

Mindfulness Tip: *Stop eating well before you're full. It takes 20 minutes to digest food, so be mindful of your pace. The more slowly you eat, the more easily you will be able to discern when you're truly satisfied.*

SPICY TURMERIC–PEPPER TEA

PREP TIME: 8 MINUTES / COOK TIME: 10 MINUTES

Although decaffeinated, this zesty tea makes a fantastic alternative to your morning coffee, thanks to a trifecta of zesty warming spices: ginger, black peppercorns, and cloves. Make another batch in the afternoon for a midday pick-me-up for the mind, body, and spirit.

5 cups water

1 (2-inch) ginger knob, peeled

1 tablespoon cardamom seeds

1 tablespoon black peppercorns

¼ teaspoon saffron

1 teaspoon turmeric

2 tablespoons cloves

1 tablespoon raw honey

1. In a medium pot, boil the water, ginger, cardamom seeds, peppercorns, saffron, turmeric, and cloves for 5 minutes.

2. Remove from the heat and let stand for another 5 minutes.

3. Stir in the honey and serve.

KAPHA

2–4
SERVINGS

SEASONS: LATE
WINTER/SPRING

TASTES: ASTRINGENT,
BITTER, PUNGENT,
SOUR, SWEET

Vatas *can substitute mint for the saffron.*

Pittas *can substitute fennel, peppermint, and star anise for the ginger, black peppercorn, and cloves.*

Kaphas *can increase the ginger for more uplifting flavor and go lighter on the honey.*

Ayurvedic Lifestyle Tip: *Moisturize your body using oils, such as olive, coconut, or mustard seed, instead of lotion. Massaging the oil into your skin rejuvenates muscles, increases circulation, reduces fatigue, and increases hydration.*

CINNAMON-ALMOND CHAI

PREP TIME: 8 MINUTES / COOK TIME: 10 MINUTES

VATA

1
SERVING

SEASON: FALL

TASTES: ASTRINGENT, BITTER, PUNGENT, SALTY, SOUR, SWEET

Vatas *can add fennel for more digestive support and use cow's milk.*

Pittas *can substitute fennel and peppermint for the ginger and cloves and can omit or reduce the honey. They can also substitute hemp, rice, or soy milk for the almond milk.*

Kaphas *can go lighter on the honey.*

Almond milk works beautifully in this twist on traditional dairy-based chai. With all the warm, delicious spices, you won't taste the difference. It's also easier to digest without the dairy.

4 cups water
6 cardamom pods, crushed
4 cloves
3 star anise pods
2 cinnamon sticks
1 (1-inch) ginger knob
Pinch salt
1 cup almond milk
1 teaspoon raw honey

1. In a medium pot, boil the water, cardamom, cloves, star anise, cinnamon, ginger, and salt for 5 minutes.

2. Remove from the heat and let stand for another 5 minutes.

3. Stir in the almond milk and honey.

4. Strain the chai into a cup and enjoy.

Timesaving Tip: *Premeasure the ingredients in your meals to streamline cooking. This prevents you from getting sidetracked while preparing food, overlooking or mismeasuring ingredients, or becoming stressed. All this equals less time slaving over the stove and more time enjoying what you've made.*

SPICED HONEY CHAI WITH STAR ANISE

PREP TIME: 8 MINUTES / COOK TIME: 10 MINUTES

For lazy winter days or cool, damp spring mornings, warm up with this invigorating comfort food in a cup. It's got all the kick a kapha needs to get up and moving on idle, cold-weather mornings.

4 cups water

6 cardamom pods, crushed

4 cloves

3 star anise pods

2 cinnamon sticks

1 (1-inch) ginger knob

1 tablespoon fennel seeds

1 teaspoon black tea

1 cup almond milk

1 teaspoon raw honey

1. In a medium pot, boil the water, cardamom, cloves, star anise, cinnamon, ginger, fennel seeds, and black tea for 5 minutes.

2. Remove from the heat and let stand for another 5 minutes.

3. Stir in the almond milk and honey.

4. Strain the chai into a cup and enjoy.

Mindfulness Tip: *Smell your food as it's cooking and while you eat to keep yourself in the moment. Plus, aromatic and flavorful scents can trick your brain into thinking you've already eaten, so you ultimately feel fuller sooner and eat less this way.*

KAPHA

1
SERVING

SEASONS: WINTER/ EARLY SPRING

TASTES: ASTRINGENT, BITTER, PUNGENT, SALTY, SOUR, SWEET

Vatas *can add fresh mint for more digestive support and omit the black tea.*

Pittas *can omit or reduce the black tea, star anise, ginger, and honey. Instead, try saffron, peppermint, or fresh basil. They should also substitute hemp, rice, coconut, or soy milk for the almond milk.*

Kaphas *can go lighter on the honey.*

VANILLA COCOA CHAI

PREP TIME: 8 MINUTES / COOK TIME: 10 MINUTES

PITTA

1

SERVING

SEASON: SUMMER

TASTES: BITTER,
PUNGENT, SWEET

Vatas *can substitute almond milk for the coconut milk.*

Pittas *can add a touch of maple syrup to sweeten.*

Kaphas *can substitute almond milk for the coconut milk and add a touch of raw honey to sweeten.*

Vanilla, cocoa, and coconut make this sweet summertime treat a wonderful coolant for the pitta energies. Serve this chai warm, not scalding hot, to avoid heating the body and fueling the pitta nature.

4 cups water
6 cardamom pods, crushed
1 or 2 vanilla beans
1 cinnamon stick
1 tablespoon fennel seeds
1 cup coconut, rice, soy, or hemp milk
3 tablespoons cacao nibs

1. In a medium pot, boil the water, cardamom, vanilla, cinnamon, and fennel seeds for 5 minutes.

2. Remove from the heat and let stand for another 5 minutes.

3. Stir in the coconut milk and cacao nibs.

4. Strain the chai into a cup and enjoy.

Ayurvedic Lifestyle Tip: *Boost hydration, prevent hair loss, and reinvigorate your mood with an oil massage for your hair and scalp. Rub olive, coconut, or mustard seed oils into your hair and scalp for two to three minutes, then leave in overnight for ultraconditioning.*

MINTED MANGO LASSI

PREP TIME: 3 MINUTES

This digestif makes the perfect ending to a meal, an easy light breakfast, or a quick midday pick-me-up. While plain yogurt isn't recommended for kapha and pitta doshas, almond and coconut milks or soy yogurt are ideal alternatives.

1 mango, peeled and pitted
1 cup plain or soy yogurt
3 cups water
1 handful fresh mint

1. In a blender, blend the mango, yogurt, water, and mint until smooth.

2. Pour into 2 glasses and serve.

VATA   PITTA   KAPHA

2
SERVINGS

SEASONS: ALL SEASONS

TASTES: PUNGENT, SOUR, SWEET

Vatas *can add a touch of sea salt.*

Pittas *can substitute soy yogurt or coconut milk for yogurt and add a pinch of saffron, rosewater, or fennel.*

Kaphas *can substitute soy yogurt and add grated ginger, red chili flakes, or black peppercorns.*

Timesaving Tip: *There should be one place that holds your calendar, whether it's an old-school planner or scheduler or a high-tech tablet, smartphone, or computer.*

3

BALANCED BREAKFASTS

SPICED OATMEAL WITH ALMONDS AND FLAXSEED

PREP TIME: 2 MINUTES / COOK TIME: 13 MINUTES

VATA

2
SERVINGS

SEASONS: ALL SEASONS

TASTES: ASTRINGENT, PUNGENT, SWEET

Vatas *can add a touch of sea salt.*

Pittas *can substitute almond milk for cow's milk as well as cream of wheat for the oatmeal and/or add pitta-balancing fruit like figs, mangoes, raisins, or prunes. They should also omit the ginger and go easy on the honey.*

Kaphas *can substitute buckwheat soaked over-night in almond milk and add more ginger.*

Warm stovetop oatmeal is the perfect wake-me-up breakfast for heat-seeking vata types. Although this recipe is ideal for fall and winter, vatas can make this year-round by updating it with fresh farmers' market fruits that support this dosha.

1 cup oats
3 cups cow's milk (or 1:1 ratio of water and milk)
½ teaspoon ground cardamom
½ teaspoon ground cinnamon
½ teaspoon ground ginger
1 banana, sliced
1 tablespoon chopped almonds
2 teaspoons flaxseed
Honey, for sweetening

1. In a small saucepan, bring the oats, milk, cardamom, cinnamon, and ginger to a boil. Simmer for 4 to 5 minutes.

2. Add the banana and the almonds.

3. Simmer for an additional 4 to 5 minutes, until the fruit and the milk are absorbed.

4. Remove from the heat and top with the flaxseed.

5. Add the honey to sweeten as desired and serve.

> **Mindfulness Tip:** *When you're stressed, inhale to the count of three and exhale to the count of six. Notice your breath, the expansion of your lungs, and the sound of air traveling into your body. This keeps you present while calming you at the same time.*

ROASTED COCONUT–SESAME OATS WITH CHERRIES

PREP TIME: 3 MINUTES / COOK TIME: 20 MINUTES

Pittas love the stimulating, satisfying, nourishing properties of oatmeal—the perfect start to a demanding, competitive day. The warm temperatures can be aggravating to the pitta energy, so in the summer, serve this cool or room temperature rather than straight from the stove.

1 cup oats

3 cups almond milk

½ cup unsweetened coconut flakes

¼ cup sesame seeds

1 cup cherries, halved and pitted

1. In a small saucepan, bring the oats and almond milk to a boil.

2. Turn down the heat and simmer until the almond milk is absorbed into the oats, about 15 minutes.

3. In a small skillet over medium heat, dry toast the coconut flakes and sesame seeds until they brown, about 1 to 2 minutes.

4. Remove from the heat.

5. When the oatmeal is finished, top with the coconut, sesame seeds, and cherries and serve.

> **Ayurvedic Lifestyle Tip:** *Consistent daily exercise is fundamental to an Ayurvedic lifestyle to ward off disease, improve immunity, balance mood, combat stress, and increase flexibility and mobility. Yoga is one option, but walking, strength training, and other cardiovascular and muscle conditioning workouts count, too.*

PITTA

2

SERVINGS

SEASON: SUMMER

TASTES: ASTRINGENT, BITTER, SALTY, SOUR, SWEET

Vatas *can substitute heavier fruits like figs or dates for the cherries.*

Pittas *can add extra coconut flakes or cherries.*

Kaphas *can switch out the coconut flakes for cacao nibs, berries, or honey.*

VANILLA–ALMOND CREAM OF WHEAT WITH MANGOES

PREP TIME: 2 MINUTES / COOK TIME: 6 MINUTES

PITTA

2–4
SERVINGS

SEASON: SUMMER

TASTES: ASTRINGENT, BITTER, PUNGENT, SALTY, SWEET

Vatas *can substitute cow's milk in place of almond milk for more protein.*

Pittas *can add more mangoes or cinnamon.*

Kaphas *can add molasses or honey to sweeten.*

When outside temperatures begin soaring, pitta personalities can get equally heated. Try balancing those strong emotions with food that's nourishing to your hunger, nurturing to any mercurial emotions, and soothing to your internal demands.

1½ cups almond milk
2 tablespoons vanilla extract
2 tablespoons maple syrup
2 cups cream of wheat
2 tablespoons chia seeds
1 tablespoon ground cinnamon
1 mango, peeled, pitted, and diced

1. In a medium saucepan over medium heat, bring the almond milk, vanilla, and maple syrup to a boil.

2. Reduce the heat to low and add the cream of wheat.

3. Simmer until thickened, about 2 to 3 minutes.

4. Sprinkle with the chia seeds, cinnamon, and mango and serve.

Timesaving Tip: *Squeeze lemons, limes, or oranges into your ice cube trays and freeze. Once frozen, transfer them to a plastic bag for storage, and you've got ready-to-use, one-tablespoon servings of citrus. Simply toss them into recipes as you need them.*

TAHINI-HONEY PUFFS WITH CINNAMON PEARS

PREP TIME: 3 MINUTES / COOK TIME: 3 MINUTES

Pungent, sticky, warm, and stick-to-your-ribs hearty, this breakfast soothes, stimulates energy, and kick-starts stamina—all in one bowl. Play around with the milk options depending on your dosha type, and change up the fruits depending on what's available near you.

2 cups almond or rice milk
1 pear, peeled, cored, and sliced
1 tablespoon ground cinnamon
2 tablespoons tahini
1 tablespoon raw honey
2 cups puffed rice cereal

1. In a small saucepan over medium heat, heat the almond milk.

2. In a small bowl, dust the pear slices with the cinnamon and set aside.

3. When the milk is warm, add the tahini and honey to the milk and stir to combine.

4. In a medium bowl, pour the mixture over the cereal.

5. Top with the cinnamon-dusted pears and enjoy.

KAPHA

1

SERVING

SEASON: SPRING

TASTES: ASTRINGENT, BITTER, PUNGENT, SALTY, SWEET

Vatas *can substitute mangoes or apricots for the pears.*

Pittas *can omit or reduce the honey.*

Kaphas *can add fresh grated ginger for even more support.*

Mindfulness Tip: *Do you have a song that instantly puts a smile on your face or a spring in your step? If so, keep it on standby. When things get hectic at work or home, cue up your song and sing along. This will get you out of the funk and back to the present.*

WARM HAZELNUT GRANOLA WITH YOGURT

PREP TIME: 10 MINUTES / COOK TIME: 15 MINUTES

VATA

2–4
SERVINGS

SEASON: FALL

TASTES: ASTRINGENT, BITTER, PUNGENT, SALTY, SOUR, SWEET

Vatas *can add a touch of sea salt.*

Pittas *can substitute pump-kin seeds for the hazelnuts and soy milk instead of the yogurt. Serve room tempera-ture rather than hot from the oven.*

Kaphas *can add dried fruit and serve with soy milk instead of the yogurt.*

Homemade granola is easier than you might think, and it is ideal for all three doshas because it can be customized to your taste preferences, energy needs, and season. Vatas need to avoid adding dried fruit, but most other fruits and spices work well.

1⅔ cups oats
¼ cup almond milk
1½ tablespoons maple syrup
1½ tablespoons flaxseed
1 tablespoon coconut, almond, or olive oil
1 teaspoon ground cardamom
1 teaspoon ground cinnamon
¼ cup chopped hazelnuts
¼ cup chopped fresh dates or figs (not dried)
2 cups plain yogurt

1. Preheat the oven to 400°F.

2. In a medium bowl, stir together the oats, almond milk, maple syrup, flaxseed, oil, cardamom, cinnamon, hazelnuts, and dates until well combined.

3. On a baking sheet, spread the mixture and bake until golden, about 15 to 20 minutes.

4. Serve warm with the yogurt.

PISTACHIO–BANANA PANCAKES WITH CARDAMOM

PREP TIME: 5 MINUTES / COOK TIME: 10 MINUTES

Heavy, sweet, and sure to stick to your ribs, this healthy pancake recipe gives vata types all the energy they need to start the day. Cardamom is tridoshic, and the flours can easily be substituted to accommodate the other doshas.

1 teaspoon baking powder

½ teaspoon ground cardamom

½ teaspoon ground ginger

½ teaspoon ground cinnamon

½ teaspoon ground nutmeg

1 cup chopped pistachios

2 tablespoons brown sugar

2 cups spelt flour

1 banana

1 teaspoon vanilla extract

2 cups low-fat milk

2 tablespoons butter, melted

2 tablespoons butter or coconut oil for cooking

Molasses, for topping

1. In a small bowl, mix the baking powder, cardamom, ginger, cinnamon, nutmeg, pistachios, brown sugar, and flour.

2. In a medium bowl, mash the banana, then mix in the vanilla, milk, and butter.

3. Whisk until well blended.

4. Add the dry ingredients to the wet and stir to combine.

5. In a griddle over medium heat, melt the butter or coconut oil.

RECIPE CONTINUES ON NEXT PAGE

VATA

2–4
SERVINGS

SEASONS: FALL/WINTER

TASTES: ASTRINGENT, PUNGENT, SALTY, SWEET

Vatas *can add lemon zest and salt.*

Pittas *can switch the spelt flour to barley, oat, or wheat flour and add almonds and dates. They can also use coconut oil instead of butter and omit the warming spices like ginger, cinnamon, and nutmeg. Water or almond milk can be used instead of the low-fat milk.*

Kaphas *can switch the spelt flour to corn or buckwheat flour as well as add berries and black pepper for an energy boost. They can also use almond oil instead of butter, and water or almond milk can be used instead of the low-fat milk.*

6. Ladle ⅛ to ¼ cup of the batter onto the griddle and cook until one side is brown, about 2 minutes (the batter will bubble). Then, use a spatula to flip.

7. Cook the other side for another 2 minutes, or until brown.

8. Using the spatula, move the pancake to a plate.

9. Repeat with the remaining batter.

10. Serve with the molasses.

Mindfulness Tip: *Think about times when you normally zone out, like walking the dog, brushing your hair, or doing the dishes. Next time you do that activity, notice what you feel, see, hear, or smell in the moment. Walking the dog, you feel your feet in your shoes or your hand on a leash, you smell the fresh air, you hear traffic driving by or the breath of your dog as she runs. Staying alert to your experience as it happens keeps you in the moment.*

BLUEBERRY–LEMON CORNCAKES WITH HONEY

PREP TIME: 8 MINUTES / COOK TIME: 5 MINUTES

Kaphas love their comfort food. To stay balanced, you have to incorporate some ingredients that inspire, excite, and motivate your mind, body, and spirit. This is especially true during the late winter and early spring months, notorious for cold, damp weather.

3 eggs

1 cup buttermilk or goat's milk

1 cup cornmeal

1 cup corn flour

Zest of 1 lemon

¼ teaspoon salt

½ teaspoon baking soda

1½ teaspoons baking powder

2 tablespoons brown sugar

1 cup blueberries

2 tablespoons coconut oil

Molasses or honey, for sweetening

1. In a small bowl, whisk the eggs with the buttermilk.

2. In a medium bowl, mix together the cornmeal, corn flour, lemon zest, salt, baking soda, baking powder, and sugar.

3. Add the egg-buttermilk mixture into the dry ingredients and stir gently. Add the blueberries.

4. In a large skillet over medium heat, heat the coconut oil. When hot, spoon ¼-cup dollops of batter into the pan and cook until bubbles form on the batter and the side is browned, about 3 minutes.

5. Using a spatula, flip and cook until the other side is browned, about 2 minutes.

6. Serve with honey or molasses.

KAPHA

2–4
SERVINGS

SEASON: SPRING

TASTES: ASTRINGENT, PUNGENT, SALTY, SOUR, SWEET

Vatas *can substitute oat flour for the corn flour and use rice or wheat flour in place of the cornmeal to minimize the corn.*

Pittas *can substitute cherries for the blueberries and omit the lemon zest.*

Kaphas *can add fresh grated ginger for even more support.*

HERBED FRITTATA WITH SPRING PEAS AND ARUGULA

PREP TIME: 3 MINUTES / COOK TIME: 12 MINUTES

VATA

4–6
SERVINGS

SEASON: FALL

TASTES: ASTRINGENT, BITTER, PUNGENT, SALTY, SOUR, SWEET

Vatas *can add more herbs or a touch more sea salt to finish.*

Pittas *can switch to egg whites, omit the cheese, and incorporate more astringent herbs like parsley, saffron, fennel fronds, and dill.*

Kaphas *should eat eggs sparingly. If you indulge, add a grind of extra black pepper for some zing.*

Eggs provide just enough warmth, heaviness, and fuel to support the energetic vata energies. Make this healthier by adding an assortment of fresh farmers' market vegetables—cooked, of course.

8 eggs
½ cup shaved Parmigiano-Reggiano cheese
4 cups chopped arugula
2 cups spring peas (can use sugar snap peas or English peas, shelled)
¾ cup mixed fresh herbs (basil, cilantro, oregano, thyme)
Sea salt
Freshly ground black pepper
2 tablespoons butter or coconut oil, divided
1 onion, diced
1 garlic clove, minced
Fresh spring peas and arugula to garnish

1. In a small bowl, whisk the eggs with the cheese, arugula, peas, and herbs. Season with the salt and pepper.

2. In a large pan over medium heat, melt 1 tablespoon of butter. Add the onions and garlic, and cook for 2 minutes.

3. Pour in the egg mixture and cook until the eggs begin to set, about 5 to 8 minutes.

4. Using a spatula, lift the eggs so the uncooked parts flow to the pan and cook for 2 minutes.

5. In a smaller pan, heat the remaining 1 tablespoon of butter.

6. Put the smaller pan over the larger pan that's cooking the eggs and flip the eggs into the smaller pan.

7. Cook the other side until browned, about 3 minutes.

8. Garnish with fresh peas and arugula, if desired.

EGG WHITE SCRAMBLE WITH MUSHROOMS, ASPARAGUS, AND CILANTRO

PREP TIME: 3 MINUTES / COOK TIME: 8 MINUTES

This versatile recipe contains ingredients that are easy to find all year round. Be sure to mix it up in the summer—when fiery pittas need extra support to balance the heat—with fresh farmers' market vegetables and herbs.

2 tablespoons butter or coconut oil
½ bunch asparagus, trimmed and diced
1 cup chopped mushrooms
1 cup fresh cilantro, chopped
8 eggs, whites only
Sea salt
Freshly ground black pepper

1. In a large skillet over medium heat, melt the butter and add the asparagus, mushrooms, and cilantro.

2. Sauté for 2 to 3 minutes.

3. Add the egg whites and scramble until fully cooked, about 4 to 5 minutes.

4. Season with the salt and pepper.

Ayurvedic Lifestyle Tip: Home-cooked meals are more conducive to a healthy lifestyle because you're better able to control your ingredients and create a peaceful, calm, enjoyable setting that allows you to focus on the meal and your dinner companions.

PITTA

4
SERVINGS

SEASON: SUMMER

TASTES: ASTRINGENT, BITTER, PUNGENT, SALTY, SWEET

Vatas *can add more cilantro or salt or some basil, thyme, spinach, tomatoes, or onion.*

Pittas *can add more astringent herbs like parsley, saffron, fennel fronds, and dill.*

Kaphas *should eat eggs sparingly. If you indulge, add an extra grind of black pepper for some zing.*

ORANGE–DATE BREAKFAST SMOOTHIE

PREP TIME: 5 MINUTES

PITTA

1

SERVING

SEASON: SUMMER

TASTES: ASTRINGENT, BITTER, PUNGENT, SALTY, SWEET

Vatas can substitute cow's milk for the almond or coconut milk and a banana for the orange. Warm the milk on the stovetop prior to blending for a warmer shake.

Pittas can add ice cubes to the blender for extra cooling.

Kaphas should use almond or rice milk and add honey or maple syrup to sweeten. Warm the almond or rice milk on the stovetop prior to blending for a warmer shake.

The super-demanding, ultracompetitive need a cooling yet powerful way to start the day to fuel their fire without pushing them out of balance. A cold smoothie is just what the doctor ordered.

1 cup almond or coconut milk

1 orange, peeled

2 cups kale

6 dates, pitted

2 tablespoons flaxseed

1. In a blender, blend the almond milk, orange, kale, dates, and flaxseed until smooth.

2. Pour into a glass and enjoy.

Timesaving Tip: *Pack your bags (gym, work, school, or travel) the night before you need them. Not only will you streamline your morning, you'll also be less likely to forget something and more likely to create a stress-free a.m.*

ALMOND–DATE POWER SHAKE

PREP TIME: 3 MINUTES / COOK TIME: 3 MINUTES

You don't need fancy protein powders or expensive ingredients to make a power shake at home. This recipe gets its protein from milk and almonds, plus an energy boost from dates and banana.

2 cups skim milk
12 pitted dates
1 banana
¼ cup raw almonds

1. In a small saucepan over medium heat, heat the milk.

2. In a blender, blend the milk, dates, banana, and almonds until smooth.

3. Pour into glasses and serve.

VATA

2–4
SERVINGS

SEASONS: SPRING/SUMMER

TASTES: SALTY, SWEET

Vatas *can add a pinch of sea salt or flaxseed for more support.*

Pittas *should serve this shake cool or at room temperature and substitute almond or coconut milk for the cow's milk.*

Kaphas *should substitute almond or soy milk for the cow's milk plus turmeric, ginger, cinnamon, or other warming spices.*

Mindfulness Tip: *Resist the temptation to compare yourself to someone else, whether in success, looks, or material possessions, as doing so prevents you from being able to celebrate your own life. When you find yourself noticing what someone else has that you don't, check in with yourself. If there's a step you can take right now to move yourself closer to a goal, take it. Otherwise, take a moment to celebrate one thing you love about yourself to bring you back to the moment.*

WATERMELON–MINT POWER BREAKFAST

PREP TIME: 5 MINUTES

PITTA

1

SERVING

SEASON: SUMMER

TASTES: ASTRINGENT, PUNGENT, SALTY, SWEET

Vatas *can substitute cow's milk for the almond milk and a banana for the orange. Omit the ice cubes and warm the almond milk on the stovetop prior to blending for a warmer shake.*

Pittas *can add extra ice cubes to the blender for more cooling.*

Kaphas *should use peaches, berries, or mango instead of the watermelon. They should also use almond or rice milk and add honey or maple syrup to sweeten. Omit the ice cubes and warm the almond milk prior to blending for a warmer shake. Consider adding cinnamon or ground ginger for zest.*

This naturally protein-packed smoothie is ultrarefreshing, too, thanks to the addition of juicy watermelon and uplifting mint leaves. It's the perfect kick start when you need something fast, easy, and energizing without the heaviness of a typical smoothie.

3 cups watermelon, seeded and chopped
5 or 6 mint leaves
½ cup almond milk
2 tablespoons almond butter
1 to 2 cups ice cubes

1. In a blender, blend the watermelon, mint, almond milk, almond butter, and ice cubes until smooth.

2. Pour into a glass and enjoy.

Ayurvedic Lifestyle Tip: *Boost your immune system and sidestep flu season without a hitch by getting enough vitamin C. Ayurvedic medicine recommends amalaki, a vitamin C-packed herb that restores your vitality. Look for it in powder form at health food stores.*

STRAWBERRY-PEACH MORNING SHAKE

PREP TIME: 5 MINUTES / COOK TIME: 3 MINUTES

This warm take on a typical smoothie has all the sweetness kapha doshas crave with the spices that will get them up and moving. Keep things interesting by mixing up the spices and fruits to maximize seasonality and flavor excitement.

½ cup rice, soy, or almond milk

½ cup figs, pitted

1 peach, pitted

1 cup strawberries

1 teaspoon flaxseed

⅛ teaspoon turmeric

⅛ teaspoon ground nutmeg

⅛ teaspoon ground cinnamon

1. In a small saucepan over medium heat, heat the rice milk.

2. In a blender, blend the milk, figs, peach, strawberries, flaxseed, turmeric, nutmeg, and cinnamon until smooth.

3. Pour into a glass and enjoy.

KAPHA

1

SERVING

SEASON: SPRING

TASTES: ASTRINGENT, BITTER, PUNGENT, SALTY, SWEET

Vatas *can use cow's milk for more protein.*

Pittas *can substitute cherries for the strawberries and avocado or mango for the peach. They should also use cold milk, not warmed, and consider adding ice cubes to the blender for extra cooling in the summer months.*

Kaphas *can add ginger for even more support.*

Timesaving Tip: *When making spice blends, pastes, or salad dressings, double or triple the recipe, seal, and store in the fridge for use the following week. Most recipes will last two to three weeks, depending on the ingredients and how well you seal it.*

POMEGRANATE DETOX SMOOTHIE WITH SUNFLOWER AND GINGER

PREP TIME: 5 MINUTES

KAPHA

1

SERVING

SEASON: SPRING

TASTES: ASTRINGENT, BITTER, PUNGENT, SALTY, SWEET

Vatas *can substitute mangoes and mango nectar for the pomegranate seeds and the pomegranate juice.*

Pittas *can substitute cherries, avocado, or figs for the apple. They should also omit the ginger and consider adding ice cubes to the blender for extra cooling in the summer months.*

Kaphas *can add ginger for even more support.*

The spring and fall transition months are a great time to "detox" by using antioxidant-rich, detoxifying fruits and spices to kick-start your metabolism and get your body ready for the new season. This recipe is perfect to balance kapha when you need the most support.

1 apple, cored and sliced

1 cup pomegranate juice

¼ cup pomegranate seeds

½ cup sunflower seeds

1 (1-inch) ginger knob, peeled

1 teaspoon coconut oil

1 teaspoon raw honey

⅛ teaspoon turmeric

⅛ teaspoon ground cinnamon

⅛ teaspoon ground cardamom

1. In a blender, blend the apple, pomegranate juice, pomegranate seeds, sunflower seeds, ginger, coconut oil, honey, turmeric, cinnamon, and cardamom until smooth.

2. Pour into a glass and enjoy.

Ayurvedic Lifestyle Tip: *When you wake (and before your morning cup of coffee), drink a glass of warm water with the juice of ½ a lemon to prevent toxin buildup in your system, rid your digestive tract of impurities, and keep your energy channels flowing. Too tart? Try a teaspoon of honey in room-temperature water instead.*

STEWED APPLES WITH GINGER AND CLOVE

PREP TIME: 5 MINUTES / COOK TIME: 8 MINUTES

Stewed apples spiked with metabolism-boosting ginger and cloves make an ideal way to start the day in the cool months. They're also fantastic as an accompaniment to cornmeal pancakes, buckwheat, cream of wheat, or oatmeal. Try them with the Blueberry-Lemon Corncakes with Honey (page 63).

2 tablespoons almond or corn oil

2 or 3 apples, peeled, cored, and chopped

2 tablespoons minced fresh ginger

10 whole cloves

½ cup rice milk

1. In a medium saucepan over medium heat, heat the oil and cook the apples for 3 to 4 minutes.

2. Add the ginger, cloves, and milk and cook until the apple is soft, about 3 to 4 minutes.

3. Remove the cloves and serve.

KAPHA

2
SERVINGS

SEASON: SPRING

TASTES: ASTRINGENT, PUNGENT, SALTY, SOUR, SWEET

Vatas *can substitute peaches or plums for the apples.*

Pittas *can substitute mint and cinnamon for the ginger and clove.*

Kaphas *can add fresh grated ginger for even more support.*

Mindfulness Tip: *Focus on what makes you happy when you find yourself upset. Emotions are just your reactions to events or situations, often ones that aren't happening right now. Instead, take that moment to remind yourself of what is making you happy now. Is it the friend you're having coffee with? Your child singing in the next room? The smell of coffee brewing in your pot?*

4

BAKED GOODS

NUTTY FIG GRANOLA BARS WITH CACAO NIBS

PREP TIME: 10 MINUTES / COOK TIME: 20 MINUTES

VATA

4–6
SERVINGS

SEASON: FALL

TASTES: ASTRINGENT, BITTER, PUNGENT, SALTY, SOUR, SWEET

Vatas can add a pinch of salt and a squeeze of lemon juice.

Pittas can substitute wheat and buckwheat flours and add a pinch of saffron.

Kaphas can substitute spelt and rye flours and do a 1:1 combination of oats to buckwheat. They can also add grated ginger and a drop or two of fresh chili juice or a pinch of cayenne.

Granola bars don't have to be unhealthy. This version contains healthy flours, antioxidant-rich spices, and a variety of nuts and fruits, plus they satisfy your sweet tooth thanks to the addition of superfood cacao nibs.

½ cup oat flour
½ cup wheat flour
1 teaspoon baking powder
½ teaspoon ground cinnamon
½ teaspoon ground cardamom
½ cup brown sugar
¼ teaspoon salt
½ teaspoon orange zest
¾ cup almond milk
3 fresh figs, chopped
½ cup pistachios, chopped
½ cup cacao nibs

1. Preheat the oven to 350°F.

2. In a medium bowl, mix the oat flour, wheat flour, baking powder, cinnamon, cardamom, brown sugar, and salt.

3. Mix in the orange zest and the almond milk and stir until blended.

4. Add the figs, pistachios, and cacao nibs and stir.

5. In a greased baking pan, pour in the batter and bake for 15 to 20 minutes.

6. Cool, cut into bars, and serve.

CHEWY HONEY APRICOT BARS

PREP TIME: 8 MINUTES / COOK TIME: 18 MINUTES

Vatas will love this snack recipe when the weather turns chilly, but it's also a fantastic go-to in the summer, when apricots are in season. Denser fruits, like apricots, figs, or dates, work best in lieu of dried fruits for vatas. Feel free to experiment if you're another dosha.

2 cups oats

½ cup fresh apricots, figs, or dates, chopped

½ cup chopped pistachios

½ cup shredded coconut

2 tablespoons flaxseed

½ cup almond butter

¼ cup, plus 2 tablespoons honey

1 tablespoon coconut oil

¼ teaspoon salt

1. Preheat the oven to 350°F.

2. In a small skillet over medium heat, dry toast the oats until golden brown, about 1 to 2 minutes.

3. In a large bowl, combine the oats, apricots, pistachios, coconut, and flaxseed.

4. In a small saucepan over medium heat, bring the almond butter, honey, coconut oil, and salt to a boil for about 1 minute, stirring constantly.

5. Add the heated mixture to the oats and stir to combine.

6. Press the batter into a square baking pan and bake until golden brown, about 10 to 12 minutes.

7. Cool, cut into squares, and serve.

VATA

4–6
SERVINGS

SEASONS: SUMMER/FALL

TASTES: ASTRINGENT, BITTER, SALTY, SWEET

Vatas *can add a pinch of extra salt and a dash of cinnamon.*

Pittas *can substitute sunflower or pumpkin seeds for the pistachios and halve the honey.*

Kaphas *can substitute ½ cup of cacao nibs for the shredded coconut and add 1 teaspoon of ground ginger.*

SESAME–MAPLE POWER SNACKS

PREP TIME: 8 MINUTES / COOK TIME: 20 MINUTES

VATA

4–6
SERVINGS

SEASONS: SUMMER/FALL

TASTES: ASTRINGENT, BITTER, PUNGENT, SALTY, SWEET

Vatas *can add a pinch of salt and lemon zest.*

Pittas *can substitute sunflower or pumpkin seeds for the sesame seeds and halve the maple syrup. Use hemp or plant protein for the whey protein.*

Kaphas *can substitute 1 cup of cacao nibs for the shredded coconut or ½ cup cacao nibs and ½ cup sunflower seeds. They can substitute pumpkin seeds for the sesame seeds and honey for the maple syrup. Use almond oil instead of coconut oil and hemp or plant protein for the whey protein.*

Why reach for the vending machine when you have a supply of energy-boosting, nourishing power bars at your desk? These healthy snacks give you all the kick you need to keep your dosha balanced without the hidden sugars, fats, and preservatives.

2 cups oats
1 cup figs or dates, chopped
¾ cup chopped almonds
1 cup shredded coconut
¾ cup whey protein
2 tablespoons flaxseed
1 tablespoon ground nutmeg
¼ teaspoon salt
½ cup almond butter
3 bananas
1 tablespoon vanilla extract
¼ cup maple syrup
¼ cup coconut oil
¼ cup water
½ cup sesame seeds

1. Preheat the oven to 350°F.

2. In a large bowl, stir together the oats, figs, almonds, coconut, whey protein, flaxseed, nutmeg, and salt.

3. In a medium bowl, mash the almond butter, bananas, vanilla, maple syrup, coconut oil, and water. Add more water by the tablespoon if the mixture seems dry.

4. Add the wet mixture to the oats, and stir to combine. Mix in the sesame seeds.

5. Press the batter into a baking pan (either 8-by-8-inch or 9-by-11-inch) and bake until golden brown, about 20 minutes.

6. Cool, cut into squares, and serve.

ORANGE–CHOCOLATE ZUCCHINI MUFFINS

PREP TIME: 10 MINUTES / COOK TIME: 20 MINUTES

These grown-up muffins will appeal to the pitta personality while fueling its strong physical demands with nourishing ingredients. Add a touch of protein powder or almond butter for a bigger dose of muscle-building energy.

Coconut oil spray
2 cups oat or barley flour
1½ teaspoons baking powder
½ teaspoon baking soda
½ teaspoon kosher salt
1 teaspoon ground cinnamon
1 teaspoon ground fennel
1 teaspoon ground cardamom
1 egg
¾ cup brown rice syrup
Zest and juice of 1 orange
¼ cup coconut oil
1 teaspoon vanilla extract
½ cup applesauce
1 cup grated zucchini
1 cup carob chips
1 apple, grated (or about ½ cup applesauce)
½ cup sunflower seeds

1. Preheat the oven to 400 °F.

2. Spray a muffin tin with the coconut oil spray.

3. In a medium bowl, stir together the flour, baking powder, baking soda, salt, cinnamon, ground fennel, and cardamom.

RECIPE CONTINUES ON NEXT PAGE

PITTA

6–12
MUFFINS

SEASON: SUMMER

TASTES: ASTRINGENT, BITTER, PUNGENT, SALTY, SOUR, SWEET

Vatas *can use other flours as well, like wheat or quinoa, add a pinch of salt, and switch out the sunflower seeds for chopped almonds. They can also add 1 teaspoon of ground ginger.*

Pittas *can substitute sunflower or pumpkin seeds for the sesame seeds and halve the maple syrup. Use hemp or plant protein for the whey protein.*

Kaphas *can double the maple syrup and use fruit juice concentrate for the brown rice syrup. They can also add 1 teaspoon of ground ginger.*

4. In a medium bowl, beat the egg. Add the brown rice syrup and beat until blended.

5. Mix in the orange zest, orange juice, coconut oil, vanilla, applesauce, zucchini, carob chips, apple, and sunflower seeds.

6. Stir in the dry ingredients until well incorporated.

7. Spoon the batter into the muffin tins and bake for 20 minutes.

8. Serve warm.

Mindfulness Tip: *If you catch yourself worrying about something in the future, remind yourself that you're creating stress out of a situation that doesn't exist and sabotaging your ability to be happy right now. Instead, turn your attention to what you're doing in that moment. And if there's an action you can take to prevent or address whatever is making you worry, like phoning a friend or making a doctor's appointment, do it now so you can get back to being happy.*

SAVORY SCALLION–PUMPKIN SEED MUFFINS

PREP TIME: 10 MINUTES / COOK TIME: 20 MINUTES

Savory muffins chock-full of heart-healthy, grounding, and calming ingredients make a great snack alternative for midday. They work beautifully as an accompaniment to dinner or a quick breakfast when slathered with jam or almond butter.

Coconut oil spray

2 cups oat or barley flour

1½ teaspoons baking powder

½ teaspoon baking soda

½ teaspoon kosher salt

2 teaspoons dried onion flakes

2 teaspoons garlic powder

1½ teaspoons dried dill

½ teaspoon freshly ground black pepper

1½ cups buttermilk

1 egg

½ cup coconut oil

⅓ cup chopped scallions

¼ cup cilantro

1 cup pumpkin seeds

1. Preheat the oven to 400°F.

2. Spray a muffin tin with the coconut oil spray.

3. In a medium bowl, stir together the flour, baking powder, baking soda, salt, onion flakes, garlic powder, dill, and black pepper.

4. In another medium bowl, beat the buttermilk, egg, and coconut oil until blended.

RECIPE CONTINUES ON NEXT PAGE

VATA

6–12
MUFFINS

SEASON: FALL

TASTES: ASTRINGENT, BITTER, PUNGENT, SALTY, SOUR, SWEET

Vatas *can add 1 teaspoon of ground ginger.*

Pittas *can omit the onion flakes, garlic powder, and black pepper. Instead, use ground fennel, turmeric, and cinnamon.*

Kaphas *can add 1 teaspoon of ground ginger and substitute almond milk for the buttermilk and ghee for the coconut oil.*

5. Mix in the scallions, cilantro, and pumpkin seeds.

6. Mix in the dry ingredients until well incorporated.

7. Spoon the batter into the muffin tins and bake for 20 minutes.

8. Serve warm.

Timesaving Tip: *Create a space in your home—by the door or in your office—where you keep a basket or tray of your essentials for the day, from cell phones to keys to wallets. Ensuring that your must-haves are exactly where you need them when you need them guarantees you won't lose time rummaging around for misplaced items.*

BLACK PEPPER SNACK CAKES WITH LEMON ZEST

PREP TIME: 8 MINUTES / COOK TIME: 20 MINUTES

Chewy, spicy, and sweet, these snack cakes are a healthy twist on a traditional baked good. Pack them in a tote or gym bag for a post-workout kick, a midday pick-me-up, or a fast breakfast on the go.

1 cup barley flour
1 cup rolled barley oats
1 teaspoon baking powder
½ teaspoon freshly ground black pepper
½ teaspoon ground cinnamon
¼ teaspoon salt
½ cup honey or brown sugar
¾ cup rice milk
¼ cup almond or olive oil
Zest of 1 lemon

1. Preheat the oven to 350°F.

2. In a large bowl, mix the barley flour, barley oats, baking powder, pepper, cinnamon, and salt until well incorporated.

3. Add the honey, rice milk, oil, and lemon zest and stir.

4. Press the mixture into a square baking dish and bake until golden, about 20 minutes.

5. Cut into bars, and serve.

KAPHA

4–6
SERVINGS

SEASONS: WINTER/SPRING

TASTES: ASTRINGENT, BITTER, PUNGENT, SALTY, SOUR, SWEET

Vatas *can use wheat, oat, or quinoa flours, almond or coconut milk, and regular oats for the barley oats.*

Pittas *can use wheat or oat flours and regular oats. They can also use coconut milk for the rice milk and ground fennel for the black pepper and omit the lemon zest.*

Kaphas *can add 1 teaspoon of ground ginger.*

SUN-DRIED TOMATO AND POPPY SEED BISCUITS

PREP TIME: 8 MINUTES / COOK TIME: 15 MINUTES

PITTA

12
BISCUITS

SEASON: SUMMER

TASTES: ASTRINGENT, BITTER, SALTY, SOUR, SWEET

Vatas *can add 1 tablespoon lemon juice or zest of 1 lemon.*

Pittas *can add additional cooling spices, like fennel, cardamom, or dill, for more support.*

Kaphas *can substitute ghee for the coconut oil.*

Vegan pittas will love this easy, one-bowl biscuit recipe that contains absolutely no butter or milk. The addition of sun-dried tomatoes and poppy seeds provide the perfect bitter and astringent tastes for the pitta dosha.

Coconut oil spray
2 cups oat or barley flour
1 tablespoon baking powder
½ teaspoon baking soda
¾ teaspoon kosher or sea salt
¼ cup coconut oil
1 cup almond milk
½ cup sun-dried tomatoes, drained of oil and finely chopped
1 cup poppy seeds

1. Preheat the oven to 375°F.

2. Grease a baking sheet with the coconut spray.

3. In a medium bowl, combine the oat flour, baking powder, baking soda, and salt.

4. In a small bowl, whisk the coconut oil and almond milk until well blended.

5. Pour the liquid into the bowl of dry ingredients and mix.

6. Stir in the sun-dried tomatoes and poppy seeds.

7. Drop spoonfuls of batter onto the baking sheet and bake until golden, about 15 minutes.

8. Serve warm.

GARLIC SCALLION CORNBREAD

PREP TIME: 10 MINUTES / COOK TIME: 20 MINUTES

This vata-tailored recipe is a natural pairing with kitcharis, curries, and one-bowl meals as well as recipes like pastas or salads, instead of a traditional baguette. Consider adding fresh farmers' market herbs as well to keep things interesting.

Coconut oil spray

1½ cups wheat flour

1½ cups cornmeal

2 teaspoons baking powder

2 tablespoons cornstarch

1 teaspoon sea or kosher salt

⅓ cup ghee, melted

1½ cups buttermilk

½ cup cow's milk

3 tablespoons chopped scallions

½ cup fresh chives

2 teaspoons minced garlic

1. Preheat the oven to 400°F.

2. Grease a square baking pan with the coconut oil spray.

3. In a medium bowl, combine the flour, cornmeal, baking powder, cornstarch, and salt.

4. In another medium bowl, beat the ghee, buttermilk, and cow's milk until blended.

5. Mix in the dry ingredients until well incorporated, then stir in the scallions, chives, and garlic.

6. Spread the batter into the baking pan and bake for 20 minutes.

7. Cut into squares and serve warm.

VATA

12–16
SQUARES

SEASONS: FALL/WINTER

TASTES: ASTRINGENT, BITTER, PUNGENT, SALTY, SOUR, SWEET

Vatas *can add chopped chilies or red chili flakes.*

Pittas *can add fresh herbs like dill, fennel fronds, or basil to the batter.*

Kaphas *can add fresh corn kernels for sweetness or freshly ground black pepper for zing.*

NO-CORN CORNBREAD WITH THYME

PREP TIME: 10 MINUTES / COOK TIME: 12 MINUTES

PITTA

8–9
SQUARES

SEASON: FALL

TASTES: ASTRINGENT, BITTER, PUNGENT, SALTY, SOUR, SWEET

Vatas *can add chopped chilies or red chili flakes. Use almond or coconut milk and add 1 tablespoon brown rice syrup or honey.*

Pittas *can add fresh herbs like dill, fennel fronds, or basil to the batter.*

Kaphas *can add fresh corn kernels for sweetness. Use almond or soy milk.*

These super-easy, healthy muffins are also great for balancing pitta in the summer, if you can bear to turn on the oven. Otherwise, they're a perfect addition to a fall menu served alongside beans and rice.

Coconut oil spray
1½ cups oat or brown rice flour
1 tablespoon tapioca flour
1½ teaspoons baking powder
¼ teaspoon sea salt
2 tablespoons coconut or sunflower oil
½ cup soy, coconut, or almond milk
¼ cup fresh thyme, chopped

1. Preheat the oven to 400°F.

2. Grease a muffin tin with the coconut oil spray.

3. In a medium bowl, combine the oat flour, tapioca flour, baking powder, and salt.

4. In a medium bowl, beat the coconut oil and soy milk until blended.

5. Mix in the dry ingredients until well incorporated, and stir in the thyme.

6. Pour the batter into the muffin cups and bake until golden brown, about 12 minutes.

ZESTY LEMON–GINGER SCONES

PREP TIME: 8 MINUTES / COOK TIME: 20 MINUTES

Enjoy these scones straight from the oven with a nice green or black tea, in lieu of coffee. Kaphas may want a touch of honey to satisfy the sweet tooth. These are also an unexpected addition to a main course when served with spicy lentils.

Coconut oil spray

3 cups buckwheat flour

2 teaspoons baking powder

¼ cup plus 2 tablespoons brown sugar or honey

1 tablespoon ground cinnamon

¼ teaspoon sea or kosher salt

2 tablespoons ground ginger

Zest of 1 lemon

¼ cup plus 2 tablespoons ghee or sunflower oil

2 cups almond milk

1. Preheat the oven to 350°F.

2. Grease a baking sheet with the coconut oil spray.

3. In a medium bowl, combine the buckwheat flour, baking powder, brown sugar, cinnamon, salt, ginger, and lemon zest.

4. Add the ghee and almond milk, and stir to combine.

5. Drop spoonfuls of batter onto the baking sheet and bake until golden brown, about 20 minutes.

6. Serve warm.

KAPHA

6
SCONES

SEASONS: LATE WINTER/ EARLY SPRING

TASTES: ASTRINGENT, BITTER, PUNGENT, SALTY, SOUR, SWEET

Vatas *can substitute oat, barley, or wheat flour.*

Pittas *can substitute rice, barley, or wheat flour and omit the ginger.*

Kaphas *can add freshly ground black pepper for more spice.*

STOVETOP GARLIC–CORIANDER NAAN WITH SEEDS

PREP TIME: 12 MINUTES / COOK TIME: 10 MINUTES

KAPHA

4–6
SERVINGS

SEASON: WINTER

TASTES: ASTRINGENT, BITTER, PUNGENT, SALTY, SOUR, SWEET

Vatas *can use buttermilk instead of the yogurt, cow's milk for the rice milk, and wheat, oat, or rice flours.*

Pittas *can use soy yogurt instead of the plain yogurt, or dilute the plain yogurt with water.*

Kaphas *can serve this with dinner or spread with jam or honey in the mornings for a fast, easy breakfast on the go.*

Traditional naan can be time consuming, but this quick stovetop version can soothe your cravings in under 30 minutes.

1 cup black sesame seeds

1 cup white sesame seeds

2½ cups buckwheat flour

2 teaspoons baking powder

1 teaspoon sea or kosher salt

1 cup plain yogurt

¼ cup minced garlic

¼ cup ground coriander

½ cup rice or almond milk

2 teaspoons olive or almond oil

1 cup warm water, divided

Ghee or coconut oil spray, for cooking

1. In a small bowl, combine the black and white sesame seeds.

2. In a large bowl, stir together the buckwheat flour, baking powder, and salt.

3. Add in the yogurt, garlic, coriander, rice milk, olive oil, and ½ cup of water. Knead into a dough for about 5 minutes, adding more water as necessary to prevent dough from getting too firm or sticky.

4. On a floured surface, divide the naan into six balls and allow to rest for 5 minutes.

5. Using a rolling pin, roll the balls into thin ovals.

6. In a grill pan or large skillet, melt the ghee and cook the ovals one at a time, 1 to 2 minutes per side, using a spatula to flip when each side is golden and adding more ghee to the pan.

7. Serve warm.

FENNEL CHAPATI WITH SEA SALT

PREP TIME: 8 MINUTES / COOK TIME: 8 MINUTES

Chapati make the perfect accompaniment to many Ayurvedic foods and are versatile enough to suit all three doshas, depending on the spices and flours used. This simple recipe is perfect for pittas, thanks to fennel seeds and wheat flour, and its lightness is ideal for warm weather.

4 cups wheat flour
½ cup fennel seeds
2 cups warm water
Coconut oil spray
Ghee, for topping
Sea salt (go lighter for pitta)

1. In a large bowl, mix the wheat flour, fennel seeds, and warm water until a dough forms.

2. Make 15 to 20 round, palm-size balls of dough. Using a rolling pin, roll the individual balls into thin circles.

3. In a hot griddle sprayed with coconut oil over medium heat, cook the rolled-out chapati for 1 to 2 minutes per side, flipping with a spatula.

4. Top with the ghee and season with the sea salt before serving.

Mindfulness Tip: *Start a daily meditation practice. This doesn't have to be a two-hour-a-day ritual. Start with one minute a day, breathing in and out, while noticing your breath. Gradually up that time to five minutes, then twenty minutes. The more you practice staying focused, the more easily you can bring yourself back to the moment in real-life situations when your mind races.*

PITTA

15–20
CHAPATI

SEASON: SUMMER

TASTES: ASTRINGENT, BITTER, SALTY, SWEET

Vatas *can use milk instead of the water and add lemon zest and more sea salt.*

Pittas *can add ground cardamom or a pinch of saffron.*

Kaphas *can use buckwheat flour instead of wheat and add 1 teaspoon of ground or minced fresh ginger.*

CURRIED ONION CHAPATI

PREP TIME: 8 MINUTES / COOK TIME: 8 MINUTES

KAPHA

15–20
CHAPATI

SEASONS: WINTER/SPRING

TASTES: ASTRINGENT, BITTER, PUNGENT, SALTY, SWEET

Vatas *can use milk instead of the water and barley flour instead of the buckwheat.*

Pittas *can use barley flour instead of the buckwheat and omit the garlic and onion.*

Kaphas *can add 1 teaspoon of ground or minced fresh ginger.*

The addition of a roundhouse of pungent, zesty spices and vegetables makes this chapati a perfect option for kitcharis, curries, and other Ayurvedic meals. Leftovers can be warmed and spread with sweet jams or honey for kaphas needing a fast early-morning breakfast.

4 cups buckwheat flour

¼ cup curry powder (use mild for pitta)

¼ cup garlic powder

¼ cup chili powder

Freshly ground black pepper

1 teaspoon sea salt

2 cups warm water

1 onion, minced

Coconut oil spray

Ghee to taste

Sea salt (go lighter for pitta)

1. In a large bowl, mix the buckwheat flour, curry powder, garlic powder, chili powder, black pepper, sea salt, and warm water until a dough forms.

2. Add in the minced onion and stir.

3. Make 15 to 20 round, palm-size balls of dough. Using a rolling pin, roll the individual balls into thin circles.

4. In a griddle sprayed with coconut oil over medium heat, cook the rolled-out chapati for 1 to 2 minutes per side, flipping with a spatula.

5. Top with the ghee and season with the sea salt before serving.

FENNEL–PISTACHIO CHAPATI

PREP TIME: 8 MINUTES / COOK TIME: 8 MINUTES

One of the best things about chapati is their versatility. This recipe plays to the vata dosha nature and works well in the fall/winter months; however, you can substitute any seasonal fresh herbs you can find at your local market, like rosemary, thyme, sage, or basil.

4 cups barley flour
¼ cup ground fennel
2 tablespoons paprika
1 teaspoon sea salt
2 cups warm cow's milk
1 cup chopped pistachios
Coconut oil spray
Ghee, for topping
Sea salt (go lighter for pitta)

1. In a large bowl, mix the barley flour, fennel, paprika, sea salt, and warm milk until a dough forms.

2. Add in the pistachios and stir.

3. Make 15 to 20 round, palm-size balls of dough. Using a rolling pin, roll the individual balls into thin circles.

4. In a griddle sprayed with coconut oil over medium heat, cook the rolled-out chapati for 1 to 2 minutes per side, flipping with a spatula.

5. Top with the ghee and season with the sea salt before serving.

VATA

15–20
CHAPATI

SEASONS: FALL/WINTER

TASTES: ASTRINGENT, BITTER, PUNGENT, SALTY, SWEET

Vatas *can use almonds instead of pistachios and add more grounding herbs and spices, like cardamom and nutmeg.*

Pittas *can use water instead of the milk and omit the paprika.*

Kaphas *can use water instead of the milk and buckwheat flour instead of the barley flour.*

5
SOUPS, STEWS, AND KITCHARIS

ASPARAGUS SOUP WITH BASIL AND SCALLIONS

PREP TIME: 10 MINUTES / COOK TIME: 20 MINUTES

VATA

2
SERVINGS

SEASONS: FALL/WINTER

TASTES: ASTRINGENT, BITTER, PUNGENT, SALTY, SOUR, SWEET

Vatas can add the zest of 1 lemon.

Pittas can use rice milk instead of the milk and soy yogurt instead of plain.

Kaphas can use rice milk instead of the milk, buckwheat flour instead of the oat flour, and soy yogurt instead of plain.

Asparagus is one of those amazing tridoshic vegetables that're good for vatas, pittas, and kaphas alike. With the addition of leeks, parsnips, nutmeg, and dairy, this recipe is ideally tailored to vatas. Pittas should opt for less pungent herbs, spices, and vegetables, while the kaphas can dial up even more pungency for support.

2 tablespoons coconut oil
½ cup chopped leeks (white parts only)
2 tablespoons oat or wheat flour
½ teaspoon ground nutmeg
3 cups vegetable broth, warmed
1 bunch asparagus, trimmed and chopped
½ cup parsnips, peeled and chopped
1 cup cow's milk, warm
½ cup tightly packed fresh basil leaves, chopped
½ cup chopped scallions (white parts only)
Plain yogurt, for garnish (optional)
Pinch salt

1. In a large soup pot over low heat, heat the coconut oil and sauté the leeks until soft, about 2 minutes.

2. Add the flour and nutmeg, and cook for another 2 minutes.

3. Slowly whisk in the vegetable broth.

4. Add the asparagus and parsnips. Raise the heat to medium, and bring to a boil.

5. Simmer, covered, for 15 minutes.

6. Pour the soup into a blender, along with the milk, basil, and scallions. Purée until smooth.

7. Serve with a dollop of plain yogurt (if using), a few pieces of chopped asparagus, and the salt.

VEGETABLE BEAN SOUP WITH MINT

PREP TIME: 10 MINUTES / COOK TIME: 20 MINUTES

Most beans pacify the pitta dosha, except lentils, which should be reduced in the diet when you need to balance this energy. This hearty recipe calls for kidney beans, but you can substitute any other quick-cooking dry or canned option.

4 tablespoons coconut oil or ghee
1 large onion, chopped
2 tablespoons ground cumin
2 tablespoons ground coriander
2 tomatoes, chopped
1 cup chopped cauliflower
1 cup chopped cabbage
1 cup chopped asparagus
1 cup chopped mushrooms
1 cup chopped greens
2 (14.5-ounce) cans kidney beans, drained
4 cups vegetable broth
1 large handful fresh mint, chopped
1 teaspoon sea or kosher salt

1. In a large pot over medium heat, heat the oil. Add the onions and sauté for 2 to 3 minutes.

2. Add the cumin and coriander, and stir to combine with the onions.

3. Add the tomatoes, cauliflower, cabbage, asparagus, mushrooms, greens, beans, and broth. Cook for 15 minutes.

4. Top with the mint and salt and serve.

PITTA

6–8
SERVINGS

SEASON: SUMMER

TASTES: ASTRINGENT, BITTER, PUNGENT, SALTY, SOUR, SWEET

Vatas *can omit the mushrooms, cabbage, and cauliflower and use green beans, onions, carrots, and sweet potatoes instead.*

Pittas *can substitute any combination of broccoli, Brussels sprouts, okra, potatoes, sweet potatoes, or beans.*

Kaphas *can substitute any other beans or peas for the kidney beans.*

NGER-PUMPKIN SOUP WITH LENTILS

PREP TIME: 5 MINUTES / COOK TIME: 25 MINUTES

VATA

4–6
SERVINGS

SEASONS: FALL/WINTER

TASTES: ASTRINGENT,
BITTER, PUNGENT,
SALTY, SWEET

Vatas can add a pinch of sea salt, a dollop of yogurt, and chopped fresh cilantro to garnish.

Pittas can use split peas or chickpeas instead of the lentils and halve the onions, garlic, and ginger.

Kaphas can use diced potatoes instead of the pumpkin.

Warm up during the cold weather, while pacifying vata energies, with this ginger-spiked sweet pumpkin soup. Thanks to the lentils, this spicy dish is hearty enough for an entrée portion.

2 tablespoons coconut or olive oil
1 small onion, chopped
4 garlic cloves, peeled and minced
3 tablespoons minced fresh ginger
1 teaspoon ground cumin
1 teaspoon ground coriander
1 teaspoon garam masala
1 teaspoon turmeric
1 bay leaf
1 cup lentils, any variety
1 (15-ounce) can pumpkin purée
6 cups vegetable broth

1. In a large pot over medium-high heat, heat the coconut oil, onion, and garlic. Cook until browned, about 4 minutes.

2. Add the ginger, cumin, coriander, garam masala, turmeric, and bay leaf, stirring to coat the onions and garlic.

3. Add the lentils, pumpkin, and broth.

4. Increase the flame to high and bring the soup to a boil.

5. Turn down to medium heat and simmer for 20 minutes.

6. Remove the bay leaf and serve.

CURRIED CARROT SOUP WITH TOASTED ALMONDS

PREP TIME: 5 MINUTES / COOK TIME: 25 MINUTES

Thick, rich, nourishing, and with just enough zing to jump-start the metabolism, this healthy comfort food won't leave you hungry an hour after eating. For more antioxidants, toss in a handful of spinach or other leafy greens.

2 tablespoons olive oil

1½ pounds carrots, peeled and chopped

2 onions, peeled and chopped

1 celery stalk, chopped

2 tablespoons curry powder

6 cups vegetable broth

1 cup chopped toasted almonds
    (follow walnut-toasting instructions on page 142)

Freshly ground black pepper

1. In a large soup pot, heat the oil, then add the carrots, onions, celery, and curry powder. Sauté for 5 minutes.

2. Add the broth, bring to a boil, then simmer 15 to 20 minutes.

3. Pour the soup into a blender and blend until smooth.

4. Serve with the chopped almonds and black pepper.

Timesaving Tip: *Shift your work hours if possible to avoid getting stuck in commuter traffic. Can you start an hour earlier and leave an hour earlier? Skip lunch and leave early? Work from home the first hour of the day? Discuss with your supervisor ways to make your time work better for everyone.*

KAPHA

2–4
SERVINGS

SEASONS: WINTER/SPRING

TASTES: ASTRINGENT, BITTER, PUNGENT, SALTY, SWEET

Vatas *can add a pinch of sea salt, a dollop of yogurt, and chopped fresh cilantro to garnish.*

Pittas *can use cauliflower or potatoes instead of the carrots. Omit or use mild curry powder.*

Kaphas *can add minced fresh ginger.*

ARTICHOKE SOUP WITH BEANS AND QUINOA

PREP TIME: 5 MINUTES / COOK TIME: 23 MINUTES

KAPHA

4–6
SERVINGS

SEASON: WINTER

TASTES: ASTRINGENT, BITTER, PUNGENT, SALTY, SOUR, SWEET

Vatas *can add more vinegar, a pinch of sea salt, and chopped fresh cilantro to garnish.*

Pittas *can omit the vinegar, use white rice instead of the quinoa, and halve the onions. They can also use kale instead of the artichokes.*

Kaphas *can halve the salt and use olive oil instead of coconut oil.*

If you're ambitious and have more than 30 minutes to prep dinner, use fresh, in-season artichoke hearts instead of canned. Otherwise, canned is a fine choice. Chickpeas, quinoa, and red wine vinegar round out this dosha's taste proclivities and grounding needs.

3 tablespoons coconut oil

1 cup chopped onion

½ cup chopped celery

½ teaspoon sea or kosher salt

3 garlic cloves, minced

6 cups vegetable broth

2 (15-ounce) cans artichoke hearts, drained

3 (15-ounce) cans chickpeas or mung beans (or 1½ cans each)

1 cup quinoa

1 teaspoon freshly ground black pepper

1 tablespoon red wine vinegar (vatas can use more)

2 teaspoons chopped fresh rosemary

1. In a large soup pot on medium-high heat, heat the oil. Add the onion, celery, salt, and garlic. Cook for 2 to 3 minutes.

2. Pour in the vegetable broth and bring to a boil. Reduce the heat and simmer for 10 minutes.

3. Add the artichoke hearts, beans, and quinoa.

4. Cook for another 10 minutes.

5. Stir in the black pepper, vinegar, and rosemary and serve.

LEMONY CHICKPEA SOUP WITH SPINACH

PREP TIME: 5 MINUTES / COOK TIME: 25 MINUTES

A medley of salty, sweet, and sour flavors, this soup is ideal for balancing the vata dosha, especially served hot.

3 tablespoons coconut oil

½ cup chopped onion

½ cup chopped celery

½ teaspoon sea or kosher salt

1 teaspoon ground cumin

1 teaspoon ground cardamom

1 teaspoon mustard seeds

2 tablespoons minced fresh ginger

3 garlic cloves, minced

6 cups vegetable broth

3 (15-ounce) cans chickpeas or mung beans (or 1½ cans each)

Zest of 1 lemon

3 cups spinach

1 teaspoon freshly ground black pepper

2 teaspoons chopped fresh rosemary

2 teaspoons fresh thyme

1. In a large soup pot on medium-high heat, heat the oil. Add the onion, celery, salt, cumin, cardamom, and mustard seeds. When the mustard seeds pop, after about 2 to 3 minutes, add the ginger and garlic.

2. Cook for 2 minutes.

3. Pour in the vegetable broth and bring to a boil.

4. Reduce the heat and simmer for 10 minutes.

5. Add the chickpeas and cook for another 10 minutes.

6. Stir in the lemon zest, spinach, black pepper, rosemary, and thyme and serve.

VATA

3–4
SERVINGS

SEASONS: FALL/WINTER

TASTES: ASTRINGENT, BITTER, PUNGENT, SALTY, SOUR, SWEET

Vatas *can add a pinch of sea salt and chopped fresh cilantro and a squeeze of lemon to garnish. Lentils can also be substituted for the chickpeas.*

Pittas *can omit the ginger and garlic, halve the onions, and use kale instead of the spinach.*

Kaphas *can halve the salt and use olive oil instead of coconut oil.*

MISO STEW WITH BRUSSELS SPROUTS AND ADZUKI BEANS

PREP TIME: 5 MINUTES / COOK TIME: 15 MINUTES

PITTA

4
SERVINGS

SEASON: SUMMER

TASTES: ASTRINGENT, BITTER, PUNGENT, SALTY

Vatas *can add more pungent vegetables, like onions and garlic.*

Pittas *can add more cooling fresh herbs to garnish.*

Kaphas *can add ginger, garlic, and onions along with a grind of black pepper.*

This easy pitta pacifier is rich with flavor, nutrients, and dense, filling vegetables, perfect to energize this dosha without overstuffing you. Vatas and kaphas can add spicier curry powders, chilies, or fried garlic to give this recipe a kick of heat.

6 cups vegetable broth

2 cups Brussels sprouts, halved

1 leek, chopped (white parts only)

1 cup chopped broccoli

2 (15-ounce) cans adzuki beans, drained

2 tablespoons miso dissolved in 1 tablespoon water

¼ cup fresh dill, chopped

Sea salt

1. In a large soup pot, boil the broth.

2. Reduce the heat to simmer, and add the Brussels sprouts, leek, broccoli, and beans.

3. Cook for 5 to 7 minutes.

4. Remove from the heat and stir in the miso and dill. Season with the salt and serve.

> **Mindfulness Tip:** *Schedule mindfulness breaks throughout the day. Set your alarm for a midmorning and midafternoon break. When the alarm goes off, treat yourself to a one-minute breathing exercise during which you close your eyes and focus on the sights, sounds, and activities around you.*

CHICKPEA–SQUASH STEW WITH COCONUT MILK

PREP TIME: 5 MINUTES / COOK TIME: 25 MINUTES

This soup is a great way to reset when you're feeling out of balance, especially when you're coming off a hectic work schedule, a particularly indulgent weekend, or a holiday season. It's chock-full of good-for-you ingredients and won't leave you feeling hungry or deprived of flavor.

1½ tablespoons coconut oil

1 onion, peeled and chopped (halve for pittas)

4 garlic cloves, minced

2 tablespoons minced fresh ginger

6 cups vegetable broth

1½ cups mung beans (canned or split dried for quicker cooking time)

2 cups cubed butternut squash (can use prepackaged)

2 carrots, chopped (can use prechopped)

2 (15-ounce) cans chickpeas, drained

1 tablespoon turmeric

1 tablespoon garam masala

1 (15-ounce) can coconut milk

Sea salt

VATA   PITTA

6–8
SERVINGS

SEASONS: FALL/SUMMER

TASTES: ASTRINGENT, BITTER, PUNGENT, SALTY, SWEET

Vatas *can add a dollop of yogurt to garnish.*

Pittas *can add more cooling fresh herbs, like coriander, cilantro, or fennel, to garnish.*

Kaphas *can use soy or almond milk instead of coconut milk.*

1. In a large soup pot over medium heat, heat the coconut oil. Add the onion, garlic, and ginger, and sauté for 3 to 4 minutes.

2. Add the vegetable broth and bring to a boil. Reduce the heat to simmer and add the mung beans, squash, carrots, chickpeas, turmeric, and garam masala.

3. Simmer for 20 minutes.

4. Add the coconut milk and stir to heat through.

5. Season with sea salt and serve.

FAVA BEAN STEW WITH POLENTA

PREP TIME: 5 MINUTES / COOK TIME: 25 MINUTES

KAPHA

6–8
SERVINGS

SEASON: SPRING

TASTES: ASTRINGENT,
BITTER, PUNGENT, SALTY,
SOUR, SWEET

Vatas *can use cauliflower instead of the kale, or cook the kale in the oil with the ginger.*

Pittas *can halve or omit the ginger and curry powder.*

Kaphas *can add 1 small chile pepper for heat.*

This is one of those fantastic base recipes that you can use to mix and match the flavors you love depending on the season, your dosha, and your balancing needs. Basically any vegetables can be added, from potatoes and parsnips to peas to cauliflower and broccoli to any greens fresh and readily available.

¼ cup olive oil

1 tablespoon mustard seeds

1 tablespoon minced fresh ginger

1 tablespoon hot curry powder

1 tablespoon ground coriander

1 tablespoon turmeric

1 tablespoon ground cumin

1 tablespoon ground dried thyme

1 onion, chopped

4 garlic cloves, minced

1 carrot, peeled and sliced (or preshredded packaged)

8 cups vegetable broth

1½ cups polenta

1 bunch kale, stemmed and chopped

2 (15-ounce) cans fava beans, drained

Lime or lemon wedges, for garnish

1. In a large soup pot over medium heat, heat the olive oil. Add the mustard seeds and cook until they pop, about 2 minutes.

2. Add the ginger and cook for 2 minutes.

3. Add the curry powder, coriander, turmeric, cumin, and thyme, and cook until fragrant, about 2 minutes.

4. Add the onion, garlic, and carrot, and stir to coat in the spices. Cook for 3 to 5 minutes.

5. Pour in the vegetable broth, increase the heat to high, and bring to a boil.

6. Add the polenta, lower the heat, and simmer for 10 minutes.

7. Add the kale and fava beans and cook for another 5 minutes.

8. Serve with the lime or lemon wedges.

Ayurvedic Lifestyle Tip: *Spike your meals with fresh herbs, like parsley, cilantro, thyme, rosemary, and mint, or spices like garlic, turmeric, cardamom, and cinnamon. These healthy ingredients boost immunity, combat disease, and trigger your body's metabolic processes. Not to mention, your home-cooked meals will get an incredible flavor boost.*

EGGPLANT STEW WITH TOASTED COCONUT AND MINT

PREP TIME: 5 MINUTES / COOK TIME: 22 MINUTES

KAPHA

6
SERVINGS

SEASONS: WINTER/SPRING

TASTES: ASTRINGENT, BITTER, PUNGENT, SALTY, SOUR, SWEET

Vatas can use coconut milk instead of the vegetable broth and squash for the eggplant.

Pittas can use coconut milk instead of the vegetable broth and substitute potatoes, squash, or zucchini for the eggplant.

Kaphas can add a chile or minced fresh ginger to offset the sweetness of the coconut or omit the coconut.

Enjoy this hearty soup as an appetizer or a stand-alone meal served with rice, chapati, or naan. Vatas can serve with yogurt as well. A squeeze of lemon before serving can help bring out the flavors for all doshas.

3 tablespoons ghee
1 large onion, diced
2 tablespoons ground cumin
2 tablespoons turmeric
2 teaspoons ground coriander
2 teaspoons black mustard seeds
1 tablespoon paprika
3 eggplants, peeled and chopped
3 large potatoes, chopped
1½ cups cauliflower
2 tomatoes, diced
1 (15-ounce) can vegetable broth
1½ cups unsweetened coconut flakes
Sea salt
1 handful mint, chopped

1. In a large soup pot over medium heat, heat the ghee and add the onion, cumin, turmeric, coriander, mustard seeds, and paprika. Cook for 2 to 3 minutes.

2. Add the eggplant and the potatoes and cook for 5 minutes.

3. Add the cauliflower, tomatoes, and vegetable broth, and cook for 15 to 20 minutes.

4. In a small skillet over medium heat, dry toast the coconut flakes until they brown, about 1 to 2 minutes.

5. Garnish with the coconut, sea salt, and mint and serve.

CAULIFLOWER–LENTIL STEW

PREP TIME: 3 MINUTES / COOK TIME: 16 MINUTES

Quinoa is a protein-rich addition to this nourishing, energizing, and detoxifying stew. It can be served with or without the quinoa, depending on how hearty you'd like your meal. Mung beans or chickpeas are a great alternative to the lentils.

3 tablespoons olive oil

1½ tablespoons ground cumin

1 tablespoon ground coriander

1 tablespoon ground fennel

12 cardamom pods

1 tablespoon turmeric

4 bay leaves

4 cinnamon sticks

2 tablespoons minced fresh ginger

¼ cup unsweetened coconut flakes

8 cups vegetable broth

2 cups canned or fresh lentils

1¼ cups quinoa

2 cups chopped cauliflower

1. In a large soup pot over medium heat, heat the olive oil and add the cumin, coriander, fennel, cardamom, and turmeric.

2. Add the bay leaves, cinnamon, ginger, coconut, and vegetable broth and bring to a boil.

3. Lower the heat and add the lentils, quinoa, and cauliflower.

4. Simmer for 10 to 15 minutes.

5. Remove the bay leaves and serve.

PITTA

SERVINGS

SEASONS: SUMMER/FALL

TASTES: ASTRINGENT, BITTER, PUNGENT, SALTY, SWEET

Vatas *can use squash in place of the cauliflower and add lemon or salt for flavor.*

Pittas *can use potatoes, squash, or zucchini instead of lentils and add a squeeze of lemon.*

Kaphas *can add a chili or minced fresh ginger to offset the sweetness of the coconut or omit the coconut.*

INDIAN STEW WITH TOFU AND TOMATOES

PREP TIME: 5 MINUTES / COOK TIME: 25 MINUTES

PITTA

6–8
SERVINGS

SEASON: SUMMER

TASTES: ASTRINGENT, BITTER, PUNGENT, SALTY, SOUR, SWEET

Vatas *can add chilies, mustard seeds, or garlic for heat.*

Pittas *can add quinoa for heartiness.*

Kaphas *can add mustard seeds and/or add more chilies. Also, use sunflower oil rather than coconut oil.*

This spin on chicken masala satisfies the voracious pitta appetite with its abundant use of fresh tomatoes, tofu, and cooling herbs. For a heavier meal, serve with chapati or stovetop naan—options that won't weigh you down in warm weather.

2 tablespoons coconut oil

3 tablespoons ground ginger

3 tablespoons ground cumin

3 tablespoons ground coriander

1 tablespoon turmeric

1 onion, chopped

2 (14-ounce) packages firm tofu, drained and cubed

2 (15-ounce) cans crushed tomatoes

4 cups spinach leaves

1 (15-ounce) can coconut milk

1 teaspoon salt

1 bunch fresh cilantro leaves, chopped

Orange zest, for garnish (optional)

1. In a large soup pot over medium heat, heat the oil and add the ginger, cumin, coriander, and turmeric.

2. Cook for 1 to 2 minutes and add the onion and tofu.

3. Stir to combine with the spices and cook for 10 minutes.

4. Add the tomatoes and spinach, and bring to a boil.

5. Lower the heat and add the coconut milk and salt.

6. Simmer for 10 to 15 minutes.

7. Garnish with the cilantro and orange zest (if using) and serve.

MISO KITCHARI WITH BLACK RICE AND CHILIES

PREP TIME: 5 MINUTES / COOK TIME: 25 MINUTES

Miso is one of those amazing tridoshic foods, making this recipe super easy to adapt to any dosha. This version, spiked with black rice, ginger, and chilies, plays to the vata's need for spicy, salty foods to satisfy and nurture its mind, body, and spirit.

6 cups vegetable broth

2 cups quick-cooking black rice

1 (15-ounce) can split peas, drained

1 to 2 cups vata vegetables, like spinach, mushrooms, sprouts, or snow peas (optional)

1 teaspoon sea or kosher salt

3 tablespoons ghee

3 tablespoons cumin seeds

3 tablespoons mustard seeds

4 cardamom pods

2 tablespoons turmeric

2 tablespoons minced or chopped fresh ginger

4 garlic cloves, minced or chopped

2 Thai green chilies or 1 teaspoon red chili flakes (optional)

¼ cup miso

Squeeze of 1 lemon

1. In a large soup pot over medium heat, bring the vegetable broth to a boil and add the rice.

2. Lower the heat and add the peas, vegetables, and salt. Simmer for 15 minutes.

3. In a small skillet over medium heat, heat the ghee and add the cumin, mustard seeds, cardamom, and turmeric.

RECIPE CONTINUES ON NEXT PAGE

VATA

6–8
SERVINGS

SEASON: SPRING

TASTES: ASTRINGENT, BITTER, PUNGENT, SALTY, SOUR, SWEET

Vatas *can add more chilies, mustard seeds, ginger, or garlic for heat.*

Pittas *can omit the garlic and chilies and garnish with orange zest rather than lemon juice to brighten.*

Kaphas *can add mustard seeds and/or add more chilies. Also, use sunflower oil rather than ghee.*

4. Cook for 1 to 2 minutes, or until the mustard seeds pop.

5. Add the ginger, garlic, and chilies. Stir to combine with the spices, and cook for 2 minutes.

6. Add the ghee mixture and miso to the rice and peas mixture, garnish with a squeeze of lemon, and serve.

Timesaving Tip: *E-mails and phone calls can be a time suck and a major distraction. Instead of scattering communication throughout the day, dedicate a block of time to returning correspondence, then focus the rest of your day on getting things done.*

QUINOA KITCHARI WITH CARAMELIZED RED ONIONS

PREP TIME: 4 MINUTES / COOK TIME: 24 MINUTES

Caramelized onions give this spin on kitchari a sweet, rustic flair and a bold, pungent aroma. Although it's ideal for seasons when kaphas need the most balance—late winter or early spring—it's equally delicious using summertime, straight-from-the-garden onions or leeks.

3 tablespoons sunflower oil

3 tablespoons cumin seeds

3 tablespoons mustard seeds

4 cardamom pods

2 tablespoons turmeric

2 red onions, sliced

2 tablespoons minced or chopped fresh ginger

4 garlic cloves, minced or chopped

2 Thai green chilies or 1 teaspoon red chili flakes (optional)

6 cups vegetable broth

1 cup quinoa

2 (15-ounce) cans lentils, drained

1 to 2 cups kapha vegetables, like spinach, mushrooms, or eggplant (optional)

1 teaspoon sea or kosher salt

Squeeze of 1 lemon

1. In a large soup pot over medium heat, heat the oil and add the cumin, mustard seeds, cardamom, and turmeric. Cook for 1 to 2 minutes, or until the mustard seeds pop.

2. Add the onions, ginger, garlic, and chilies (if using). Stir to combine with the spices, and cook for 8 to 10 minutes.

3. Add the vegetable broth and bring to a boil.

RECIPE CONTINUES ON NEXT PAGE

KAPHA

6–8
SERVINGS

SEASON: WINTER

TASTES: ASTRINGENT, BITTER, PUNGENT, SALTY, SOUR, SWEET

Vatas *can add more chilies, mustard seeds, ginger, or garlic for heat, cut down on the lentils, and use ghee instead of sunflower oil.*

Pittas *can halve the red onions, use coconut oil instead of sunflower, and garnish with orange zest rather than lemon juice to brighten.*

Kaphas *can add more mustard seeds and/or chilies.*

4. Add the quinoa and lower the heat.

5. Add the lentils, vegetables (if using), and salt.

6. Simmer for 15 minutes.

7. Garnish with a squeeze of lemon and serve.

Mindfulness Tip: *Start your day with a luxurious three-minute stretch. Reach your arms overhead, stretch your legs, twist your sides—notice how your body feels as you awaken it.*

SWISS CHARD KITCHARI WITH BROWN RICE

PREP TIME: 4 MINUTES / COOK TIME: 18 MINUTES

Chock-full of antioxidant-rich Swiss chard, this pungent, bitter recipe is ideal for the spring transitional season, when kaphas need the most support coming off the cold, damp winter and indulgent holiday season.

3 tablespoons sunflower oil

¼ cup cumin seeds

¼ cup fennel seeds

2 tablespoons turmeric

¼ cup minced or chopped fresh ginger

6 cups vegetable broth

1 cup quick-cooking brown rice

1 bunch chard, stemmed and chopped

1 to 2 cups kapha vegetables, like eggplant, cauliflower, onions, or potatoes (optional)

1 bunch fresh cilantro, chopped

Squeeze of 1 lime, for garnish

1. In a large soup pot over medium heat, heat the oil and add the cumin, fennel, and turmeric.

2. Cook for 1 to 2 minutes.

3. Add the ginger, and cook for another minute.

4. Add the vegetable broth and bring to a boil, then add the rice and lower the heat.

5. Add the chard and vegetables (if using), and simmer for 15 minutes.

6. Garnish with the cilantro and lime juice and serve.

KAPHA

6–8
SERVINGS

SEASON: SPRING

TASTES: ASTRINGENT, BITTER, PUNGENT, SALTY, SOUR, SWEET

Vatas *can double up on the rice and spice.*

Pittas *can double up on the cooling herbs and spices, and garnish with orange zest.*

Kaphas *can halve the rice and add heating spices, like cinnamon and freshly ground black pepper.*

SEAWEED KITCHARI WITH SESAME SEEDS

PREP TIME: 4 MINUTES / COOK TIME: 18 MINUTES

PITTA

6—8
SERVINGS

SEASON: SUMMER

TASTES: ASTRINGENT, BITTER, PUNGENT, SALTY, SWEET

Vatas *can double up on the rice and spice, halve the beans, and add mustard seeds.*

Pittas *can double up on the cooling herbs and spices, and garnish with orange zest.*

Kaphas *can halve the rice and double up on the beans and add mustard seeds, onions, and garlic.*

Asian cuisines and an abundance of greens make excellent choices for the pitta dosha, and this recipe combines both. Mung beans are well-known detoxifiers, which work alongside the anti-inflammatory spices and vitamin-packed rice to cleanse the system.

3 tablespoons olive oil or ghee

¼ cup cumin seeds

2 tablespoons turmeric

2 tablespoons minced or chopped fresh ginger

6 cups vegetable broth

1 cup quick-cooking brown rice

2 (15-ounce) cans mung beans, drained

1 cup seaweed (kombu)

1 to 2 cups pitta vegetables, like spinach, mushrooms, sprouts, or snow peas (optional)

1 bunch fresh cilantro, chopped

¼ cup toasted black sesame seeds (instructions on page 146)

1. In a large soup pot over medium heat, heat the oil and add the cumin and turmeric.

2. Cook for 1 to 2 minutes.

3. Add the ginger, and cook for another minute.

4. Add the vegetable broth and bring to a boil.

5. Add the rice and lower the heat.

6. Add the mung beans, seaweed, and vegetables (if using), and simmer for 15 minutes.

7. Garnish with the cilantro and sesame seeds and serve.

VEGETABLE KITCHARI WITH TAHINI DRIZZLE

PREP TIME: 6 MINUTES / COOK TIME: 19 MINUTES

This low-key medley of mung beans, rice, and spices eases diges-tion, improves circulation, and soothes nerves—the perfect antidote for a stressful holiday season. Or whip up a batch in the summer months using fresh local seasonal herbs and vegetables.

2 tablespoons ghee

1 tablespoon cumin seeds

1 tablespoon turmeric

1 tablespoon ground coriander

1 tablespoon freshly ground black pepper

1 tablespoon ground cinnamon

1 tablespoon ground cumin

½ tablespoon sea salt

½ tablespoon ground cloves

3 bay leaves

2 tablespoons minced fresh ginger

4 garlic cloves, minced

1 onion, diced

1 cup basmati rice

1 (15-ounce) can mung beans (or ½ cup dried split mung beans)

1 cup chopped green beans

1 cup chopped asparagus

½ cup shredded carrots

½ cup shelled peas

1 cup spinach

1 cup squash, cubed (can use prepackaged)

6 cups vegetable broth

Tahini, for drizzling

RECIPE CONTINUES ON NEXT PAGE

VATA

4–6
SERVINGS

SEASONS: ALL SEASONS

TASTES: ASTRINGENT, BITTER, PUNGENT, SALTY, SOUR, SWEET

Vatas can add lemon or more salt for flavor, or yogurt for creaminess.

Pittas can use zucchini for the carrots and halve the number of bay leaves.

Kaphas can add a chile, omit the tahini drizzle, and use cauliflower instead of the squash.

1. In a large soup pot over medium heat, heat the ghee and add the cumin seeds.

2. Cook for 1 minute.

3. Add the turmeric, coriander, black pepper, cinnamon, cumin, sea salt, cloves, bay leaves, ginger, garlic, and onion. Cook for 2 to 3 minutes.

4. Add the rice, mung beans, green beans, asparagus, carrots, peas, spinach, squash, and broth.

5. Bring to a boil.

6. Reduce the heat and simmer for 15 minutes.

7. Remove the bay leaves and serve drizzled with the tahini.

Ayurvedic Lifestyle Tip: *Treat yourself to a vase of fresh flowers in your home or office. Surrounding yourself in nature is one of the keys to staying calm and relaxed. When you're feeling stressed, focus on them—their shape, their color, their fragrance—for an instant reality check.*

SPICED KITCHARI WITH TOFU AND RED RICE

PREP TIME: 5 MINUTES / COOK TIME: 19 MINUTES

Protein-rich tofu and other soothing, nurturing ingredients make this dish like the chicken soup of Ayurvedic cooking. Tofu works best for vatas when cooked and served warm or hot.

2 tablespoons coconut oil

3 tablespoons ground ginger

3 tablespoons ground cumin

3 tablespoons black mustard seeds

1 tablespoon fennel seeds

1 tablespoon fenugreek seeds

1 tablespoon ground coriander

1 tablespoon turmeric

1 onion, chopped

2 (14-ounce) packages firm tofu, drained and cubed

2 cups leftover red rice (or quinoa if you have no leftover rice)

6 cups vegetable broth

4 cups spinach leaves

1 teaspoon salt

1 bunch fresh cilantro leaves, chopped

1. In a large soup pot over medium heat, heat the oil and add the ginger, cumin, black mustard seeds, fennel seeds, fenugreek seeds, coriander, and turmeric. Cook for 1 to 2 minutes.

2. Add the onion and tofu and stir to combine with the spices. Cook for 8 to 10 minutes.

3. Add the rice and broth, and bring to a boil.

4. Lower the heat, and simmer for 10 to 15 minutes.

5. Stir in the spinach leaves and salt.

6. Garnish with the cilantro and serve.

VATA

6–8
SERVINGS

SEASONS: FALL/WINTER

TASTES: ASTRINGENT, BITTER, PUNGENT, SALTY, SWEET

Vatas *can add chilies for additional heat.*

Pittas *can omit the ginger and garnish with mint instead of cilantro.*

Kaphas *can add chilies and use sunflower oil rather than coconut oil.*

6
VEGETABLES, GRAINS, AND LEGUMES

SPICED ASPARAGUS WITH LEMON ZEST

PREP TIME: 5 MINUTES / COOK TIME: 8 MINUTES

VATA   PITTA   KAPHA

2–4
SERVINGS

SEASON: SUMMER

TASTES: ASTRINGENT, BITTER, PUNGENT, SALTY, SOUR, SWEET

Vatas *can add a splash of balsamic vinegar for flavor.*

Pittas *can omit the curry powder and add cooling spices like dill.*

Kaphas *can add a chile or minced fresh ginger for additional kick.*

Play around with different varieties of asparagus to tailor this dish to your particular tastes and energy. For instance, white asparagus is sweeter than green, making it a nice option when you're looking to switch things up.

2 tablespoons ghee or coconut oil

1 tablespoon curry powder (adjust heat for your particular dosha)

1 bunch asparagus, trimmed

1 tablespoon freshly squeezed lemon juice

½ teaspoon sea or kosher salt

Zest of 1 lemon

1. In a pan over medium heat, heat the ghee.

2. Add the curry powder and cook for 1 to 2 minutes, until you detect its aroma.

3. Add the asparagus and lemon juice and cook until tender with a slight crisp, about 3 minutes.

4. Garnish with the sea salt and lemon zest and serve.

Timesaving Tip: *Enlist the services of handymen, lawn mowers, or errand runners to do the chores or tasks you don't have time to do. While it seems like an unnecessary expense, consider how long those obligations would take you, the value of your time, and what else needs to be done on your agenda that's more important.*

STIR-FRIED OKRA WITH CILANTRO AND PEPPERS

PREP TIME: 4 MINUTES / COOK TIME: 5 MINUTES

Okra is a tridoshic food, and the quick cooking method here keeps the crunchiness of this sometimes-hated vegetable intact. Feel free to add ginger or other heating spices to balance the vata and kapha doshas.

2 tablespoons ghee or coconut oil

2 tablespoons cumin seeds

2 to 3 Thai red chilies, deseeded

1 pound okra, sliced

1 tablespoon turmeric

¾ cup cilantro

½ teaspoon sea or kosher salt

Squeeze of lemon, for garnish

1. In a large pan over medium heat, heat the ghee. Add the cumin seeds. Cook for 1 to 2 minutes, until they pop.

2. Add the red chili and tomatoes. Cook 4 to 5 minutes.

3. Add the okra and turmeric and cook until tender with a slight crisp, about 3 minutes.

4. Garnish with the sea salt, cilantro, and lemon and serve.

VATA   KAPHA

2–4
SERVINGS

SEASON: SUMMER

TASTES: ASTRINGENT, BITTER, PUNGENT, SALTY, SWEET

Vatas *can add an extra splash of freshly squeezed lemon juice for flavor.*

Pittas *can use fennel seeds for the mustard seeds and add cooling spices like dill. Also, use a bit more freshly squeezed lemon juice instead of the salt.*

Kaphas *can add a chile or minced fresh ginger for additional kick.*

> **Mindfulness Tip:** *End your day with gratitude. Before bed, tell your partner, the dog, or a friend about five things that you were grateful for that day. You'll instantly feel the gratitude pouring back through your body as though you're experiencing it again in real time.*

PICKLED BEETS AND AVOCADO WITH FETA

PREP TIME: 5 MINUTES

VATA

2
SERVINGS

SEASONS: FALL/WINTER

TASTES: BITTER, PUNGENT, SALTY, SOUR, SWEET

Vatas *can add a grind of black pepper for flavor.*

Pittas *can substitute blanched green beans for beets.*

Kapha *can substitute chickpeas, fried potatoes, or unpickled roasted beets for pickled beets, plus add a grind of black pepper.*

This super-easy recipe takes full advantage of the spring, summer, and fall farmers' markets' handcrafted pickled options. Pickling spices and brine balance vata dosha particularly in the fall and winter. If you've got leftover roasted beets, toss in a splash of balsamic vinegar to get the same taste profile.

1 (16-ounce) jar pickled beets, quartered
1 avocado, peeled, pitted, and diced
Squeeze of 1 lemon
½ cup crumbled feta cheese

1. On 2 serving plates, divide the beets equally.

2. Add the avocado, and squeeze the lemon over the beets and avocado.

3. Sprinkle the crumbled feta over the top and serve.

Ayurvedic Lifestyle Tip: *You don't need a monthly spa appointment to reap the benefits of a fantastic massage. A five-minute self-massage when you wake, midday, or before bed increases circulation, soothes muscles, improves energy, and calms your mind. Focus on areas that seem to be holding tension—arms, neck, shoulders, or hips—and add aromatherapy oils if you're feeling indulgent.*

DINOSAUR KALE WITH GARLIC AND CURRANTS

PREP TIME: 3 MINUTES / COOK TIME: 7 MINUTES

With its abundance of antioxidants and minerals, kale brings to life one of the concepts behind Ayurveda: that food is medicine. This recipe is fast, easy, and particularly suited for vatas and kaphas or anyone looking for bountiful energy in minutes.

2 tablespoons ghee or coconut oil

2 garlic cloves, sliced thin

1 bunch kale, stemmed and chopped

¾ cup currants

Squeeze of 1 lemon

Sea salt to taste

1. In a large skillet over medium heat, melt the ghee and add the garlic.

2. Cook for 2 to 3 minutes.

3. Add the kale and currants and cook until the kale is wilted, about 5 minutes.

4. Season with the lemon and salt and serve.

VATA   KAPHA

2

SERVINGS

SEASONS: FALL/SPRING

TASTES: ASTRINGENT, BITTER, PUNGENT, SALTY, SOUR, SWEET

Vatas *can soak currants in vinegar before cooking for more support.*

Pittas *can substitute pomegranate seeds for currants.*

Kaphas *can add minced fresh ginger with the garlic when cooking.*

Timesaving Tip: *If you love your morning smoothies, but not the time it takes to make them, consider whipping up one large batch, then freezing individual servings in mason jars for the rest of the week. The night before you want to sip one, pop it in the refrigerator so it's thawed by morning.*

ASIAN FENNEL SALAD WITH MINT

PREP TIME: 5 MINUTES

PITTA

2
SERVINGS

SEASON: SUMMER

TASTES: ASTRINGENT,
BITTER, PUNGENT,
SALTY, SWEET

Vatas can substitute
cucumber for cabbage
and splash the salad with
balsamic vinegar or lemon
before serving, although
raw salads generally aren't
recommended for vatas.

Pittas can add even more
cooling fresh herbs like
cilantro.

Kaphas can add minced
fresh garlic, red chili flakes,
and scallions.

Pitta doshas love the crispy crunch and cooling aspects of a raw salad. This one uses naturally heat-defying fennel as a main component for extra balance. Cabbage, carrots, and mint further ease digestive and emotional stress.

1 large fennel bulb, trimmed and sliced thin

½ cup chopped cabbage (can use prepackaged)

1 large carrot, shredded (can use prepackaged)

1 bunch fresh mint, chopped

2 tablespoons sesame oil

1 tablespoon sunflower oil

1 tablespoon soy sauce

1. In a large bowl, toss together the fennel, cabbage, carrot, and mint.

2. In a small bowl, whisk together the sesame oil, sunflower oil, and soy sauce.

3. Pour the oil mixture over the salad and serve.

Mindfulness Tip: *Turn off the TV if you're not actively watching it. Keeping the television on as background noise encourages your mind to wander or zone out rather than keeping focused on the present.*

EGGPLANT WITH TURMERIC AND LEMON

PREP TIME: 20 MINUTES / COOK TIME: 10 MINUTES

This basic eggplant recipe serves vatas and kaphas alike and can be easily tailored to either dosha needing more balancing. For example, kaphas can add pomegranate seeds and vatas can add diced figs while cooking or before serving.

1 eggplant, diced
2 tablespoons sea salt
2 tablespoons ghee or coconut oil
2 tablespoons turmeric
Squeeze of 1 lemon

1. In a colander, sprinkle the eggplant with the salt. Let it sit for 15 minutes, then press out any excess liquid.

2. In a medium skillet over medium heat, melt the ghee. Add the eggplant and toss in the ghee.

3. Add the turmeric, and cook for 8 to 10 minutes.

4. Squeeze the lemon over the top and serve.

VATA   KAPHA

2
SERVINGS

SEASON: WINTER

TASTES: ASTRINGENT, BITTER, SALTY, SOUR, SWEET

Vatas *can use squash for the eggplant or leave in because cooking the eggplant in oil reduces some of its vata-aggravating properties.*

Pittas *can substitute Brussels sprouts for the eggplant.*

Kaphas *can add garlic.*

Ayurvedic Lifestyle Tip: *Track your progress to remind yourself that you're on a journey to better health, which comes from baby steps over time, rather than a magical overnight transformation. Refer to your journal when you need motivation to stay on track.*

BROCCOLI-CAULIFLOWER MEDLEY

PREP TIME: 10 MINUTES / COOK TIME: 15 MINUTES

PITTA

4–6
SERVINGS

SEASON: FALL

TASTES: ASTRINGENT,
BITTER, PUNGENT,
SALTY, SWEET

Vatas *can use sweet potatoes and turnips for the cauliflower and broccoli as well as add minced garlic and cayenne for heat.*

Pittas *can garnish with freshly chopped cilantro.*

Kaphas *can double the ginger and add minced garlic and cayenne for heat.*

This medley is great for the warmer fall months when using the stove isn't so appealing. Or make this in the summer, roasted on a preheated grill or sautéed stovetop in a cast iron pan.

1 head broccoli, chopped into florets
1 head cauliflower, chopped into florets
4 tablespoons olive oil
2 tablespoons turmeric
1 tablespoon minced fresh ginger
1 teaspoon sea or kosher salt

1. Preheat the oven to 425°F.

2. In a large bowl, toss the broccoli, cauliflower, olive oil, turmeric, ginger, and salt.

3. On a baking sheet, spread the broccoli and cauliflower in a single layer and roast for 15 to 20 minutes, and serve.

Timesaving Tip: *Whether it's work or play, saying "no" to obligations, unnecessary requests, or time wasters is a fast way to take back control of your schedule. Prioritizing your time over other people's demands opens up your day to your other commitments and keeps you from becoming stressed when your plate is too full.*

CURRIED CAULIFLOWER WITH MUSTARD SEEDS

PREP TIME: 3 MINUTES / COOK TIME: 7 MINUTES

This versatile, warm stir-fry pacifies the kapha energies in winter and spring but can be grilled and served room temperature in the summer with equally wonderful results. Any heating spices can be added for more balance.

2 tablespoons sunflower oil

4 tablespoons black mustard seeds

2 tablespoons curry powder (heat adjusted per dosha)

1 large head cauliflower, cut into florets (can use prepackaged)

1 teaspoon sea or kosher salt

1. In a large cast iron pan or wok over medium heat, heat the oil and add the mustard seeds. Cook until they pop, about 1 to 2 minutes.

2. Add the curry powder and sauté for 1 minute.

3. Add the cauliflower and the salt, and stir to coat the florets in the spicy oil.

4. Sauté until crisp-tender, about 5 minutes, and serve.

KAPHA

2–4
SERVINGS

SEASON: SPRING

TASTES: ASTRINGENT, BITTER, PUNGENT, SALTY

Vatas *can substitute fennel or okra for the cauliflower and dial up the curry heat.*

Pittas *can substitute coriander or fennel for the mustard seeds and use mild curry powder.*

Kaphas *can add minced fresh ginger and garlic for spice.*

Mindfulness Tip: *Multitasking is the fastest way to slip into autopilot. Instead of juggling many things at once, do one thing at a time. If you're talking on the phone, concentrate on the conversation at hand, rather than simultaneously answering e-mails, surfing the Web, and updating your to-do list.*

FARMERS' MARKET VEGETABLES WITH INDIAN SPICES

PREP TIME: 10 MINUTES / COOK TIME: 15 MINUTES

PITTA

6–8
SERVINGS

SEASONS: SPRING/SUMMER

TASTES: ASTRINGENT, BITTER, SALTY, SOUR, SWEET

Vatas *can use sweet potatoes, sweet onions, green beans, and turnips for the cauliflower, bell peppers, peas, and broccoli as well as add minced garlic and cayenne for heat.*

Pittas *can garnish with freshly chopped cilantro.*

Kaphas *can add minced garlic and cayenne for heat, and use mustard seeds for the fennel seeds.*

This roundup of in-season pitta balancers isn't just great for its naturally sweet, cooling properties (both energetically and physically) but also because it's low-stress to make and teeming with disease-fighting antioxidants.

1 cup broccoli, chopped into florets

1 cup cauliflower, chopped into florets

1 cup peas

1 cup potatoes, diced

1 cup sweet bell peppers, stemmed, seeded, and chopped

4 tablespoons olive or sunflower oil

2 tablespoons turmeric

2 tablespoons ground coriander

2 tablespoons fennel seeds

1 teaspoon sea or kosher salt

1. Preheat the oven to 425°F.

2. In a large bowl, toss the broccoli, cauliflower, peas, potatoes, bell peppers, olive oil, turmeric, coriander, fennel seeds, and salt.

3. On a baking sheet, spread the mixture in a single layer and roast for 15 to 20 minutes.

4. Serve.

Ayurvedic Lifestyle Tip: *Wild-caught fish contains numerous antioxidants, protein, and vitamins. Try to incorporate a few more servings into your diet each week in lieu of pork, red meat, shellfish, or dairy products.*

SPICED SPINACH AND POTATOES WITH LEMON ZEST

PREP TIME: 5 MINUTES / COOK TIME: 25 MINUTES

Kaphas will love this get-up-and-go, energy-boosting recipe thanks to its healthy dose of mustard seeds, minced garlic, and lemon zest. For a nice kapha-balancing crunch, top the dish with toasted sunflower or pumpkin seeds before serving.

2 tablespoons ghee or sunflower oil

2 tablespoons mustard seeds

1 tablespoon turmeric

1 tablespoon ground coriander

3 garlic cloves, minced

4 large potatoes, diced

1 large bunch spinach

1 cup vegetable broth or water

Juice and zest of 1 lemon

1½ teaspoons sea or kosher salt

1. In a large skillet over medium heat, melt the ghee and add the mustard seeds.

2. Cook until the seeds pop, about 1 to 2 minutes.

3. Add the turmeric, coriander, and garlic, and cook for 2 to 3 minutes.

4. Add the potatoes and spinach, and sauté for about 5 minutes.

5. Add the broth, lemon juice, lemon zest, and salt.

6. Cook for 15 minutes and serve.

KAPHA

4–6
SERVINGS

SEASON: SPRING

TASTES: ASTRINGENT, BITTER, PUNGENT, SALTY, SOUR, SWEET

Vatas *can use sweet potatoes for the potatoes.*

Pittas *can omit the lemon juice, substitute fennel seeds for the mustard seeds, and garnish with freshly chopped cilantro.*

Kaphas *can add cayenne for heat and ginger for digestion.*

SPICY POTATO CURRY WITH RED LENTILS

PREP TIME: 5 MINUTES / COOK TIME: 22 MINUTES

VATA

6–8
SERVINGS

SEASONS: FALL/WINTER

TASTES: ASTRINGENT, BITTER, PUNGENT, SALTY, SOUR, SWEET

Vatas *can add a dollop of yogurt or lemon zest plus chopped fresh figs or dried apricots.*

Pittas *can lessen or omit the chili powder and ginger and halve the onions and garlic. Add mint to cool.*

Kaphas *can substitute water for half of the coconut milk or use almond milk instead of the coconut milk. Add mint for sweetness.*

Spicy Middle Eastern-inspired foods are the perfect energy-balancing comfort foods when vatas feel imbalanced. The roundup of spices ensures you hit all the Ayurvedic tastes. Add raisins, figs, or apricots for more Middle Eastern flair.

3 potatoes, cubed

2 cups canned or fresh lentils

2 (14-ounce) cans coconut milk

¼ cup minced fresh ginger

¼ cup tablespoons olive oil

3 tablespoons ground chili powder

3 tablespoon cumin seeds

3 tablespoon turmeric

6 garlic cloves, minced

2 large onions, sliced

Juice of 1 lemon

1. In a large saucepan over high heat, boil the potatoes for 5 to 6 minutes. Drain.

2. In a large saucepan over medium heat, cook the lentils with the coconut milk and ginger for 10 minutes.

3. In a large skillet over medium heat, heat the olive oil and add the chili powder, cumin seeds, and turmeric. Cook for 1 minute.

4. Add the garlic, onions, and cooked potatoes, and sauté for 10 minutes.

5. Add the lentils and their broth to the spice mixture.

6. Top with the lemon juice.

CARROTS WITH RAISINS, MINT, AND LIME

PREP TIME: 5 MINUTES

This raw carrot salad is a spin-off on the traditional Indian halwa. It calls for raisins, but any dried fruit will work with the kapha dosha constitution. If you need more balancing, omit the honey—you'll still have the sweetness of the raisins.

6 to 8 carrots, peeled and grated (can use prepackaged)
1 cup raisins
2 handfuls fresh mint, chopped
Juice of 1 lime
1 tablespoon honey

1. In a large bowl, stir together the carrots, raisins, and mint.

2. In a small bowl, whisk the lime juice and honey.

3. Pour the juice-honey mixture over the carrots and serve.

KAPHA

6–8
SERVINGS

SEASON: SPRING

TASTES: ASTRINGENT, PUNGENT, SALTY, SOUR, SWEET

Vatas *can omit the raisins or substitute figs for them.*

Pittas *can substitute chopped raw Brussels sprouts or grated zucchini for the carrots and omit the honey.*

Kaphas *can garnish with sunflower seeds.*

Mindfulness Tip: *Listen when people talk to you. Really hear what they say rather than planning your response, questions, or comments. It's a more thoughtful conversation, and you're more likely to actually remember what was said because your mind isn't racing about what you have to say.*

BARLEY SALAD WITH CORN AND PUMPKIN SEEDS

PREP TIME: 3 MINUTES / COOK TIME: 20 MINUTES

VATA

4–6
SERVINGS

SEASONS: FALL/WINTER

TASTES: ASTRINGENT, BITTER, PUNGENT, SALTY, SOUR, SWEET

Vatas *can add steamed vegetables.*

Pittas *can top with raw vegetables and toasted coconut for more cooling.*

Kaphas *can add hot spices, like garlic and ginger, and omit the salt.*

For the overscheduled vata, this recipe is fast, satisfying, and easy to make in bulk. Not to mention it's simple to pack in a jar or Tupperware to take on the go.

2 cups water
½ cup pearl barley
½ cup quinoa
½ cup corn
½ cup cannellini beans
¼ cup pumpkin seeds
¼ cup olive oil
Squeeze of 1 lemon
Sea salt
Freshly ground black pepper

1. In a medium pan, boil 2 cups of water.

2. Add the barley and quinoa, and cook for 15 to 20 minutes.

3. Using a colander, drain the barley and quinoa. Return to the pan and add the corn, beans, seeds, oil, and lemon.

4. Toss, season with the salt and pepper, and serve.

Timesaving Tip: *Declutter your makeup bag by tossing out old or expired items and keeping only what you use. When your options are minimal and your products accessible, your morning beauty routine becomes fast and easy.*

LEFTOVER RICE WITH GARLICKY GREENS

PREP TIME: 5 MINUTES / COOK TIME: 12 MINUTES

Vatas will crave this take on fried rice, with its fragrant onions and garlic. While raw greens are recommended for vatas, this recipe calls for cooking them in oil before adding the rice to make them more dosha-balancing.

3 tablespoons ghee

1 large onion, chopped

5 to 6 garlic cloves, minced

6 cups greens of your choice

2 cups leftover wild, red, black, or basmati rice

1 teaspoon sea or kosher salt

1. In a large skillet over medium heat, melt the ghee and add the onion and garlic.

2. Cook until browned, about 5 minutes.

3. Add the greens, and sauté for about 5 minutes.

4. Add the leftover rice, and cook for 2 to 3 minutes to warm through.

5. Season with the salt to taste and serve.

VATA

2–4
SERVINGS

SEASON: WINTER

TASTES: ASTRINGENT, BITTER, PUNGENT, SALTY, SWEET

Vatas *can add lemon zest and top with a fried egg.*

Pittas *can halve the garlic, substitute edamame for the onion, and garnish with freshly chopped cilantro.*

Kaphas *can top with a fried egg.*

Mindfulness Tip: *Laugh. Read a comic strip, tell a joke, share a funny story. Nothing brings you back to the moment and into the happiness zone faster than a deep belly laugh.*

MINT BASMATI RICE WITH CASHEWS

PREP TIME: 3 MINUTES / COOK TIME: 20 MINUTES

PITTA

6—8
SERVINGS

SEASONS: SUMMER/
EARLY FALL

TASTES: ASTRINGENT,
PUNGENT, SALTY, SWEET

Vatas *can add onion and
ginger with the garlic.*

Pittas *can top with toasted
coconut for more cooling.*

Kaphas *can add onion and
ginger with the garlic.*

*Thanks to an abundance of mint and cashews, this simple
basmati rice recipe has all the cooling properties you'd find in
a tropical-inspired dish. For more cooling, cook the rice in half
coconut milk, half broth.*

¼ cup coconut oil
1 handful fresh mint, chopped
1 garlic clove, minced
1 cup chopped raw cashews
2 cups basmati rice
4 cups vegetable broth
1 teaspoon salt

1. In a medium pot over medium heat, heat the coconut oil. Add
the mint, garlic, and cashews, and cook for 2 to 3 minutes.

2. Add the rice and cook for 2 minutes.

3. Add the broth and salt, and bring to a boil.

4. Reduce the heat to low, cover, simmer for 15 minutes,
and serve.

Ayurvedic Lifestyle Tip: *When possible,
incorporate all six tastes (sweet, salty,
bitter, sour, pungent, astringent) into your
meal to maximize nutrients and enjoyment.*

CINNAMON–SAFFRON RICE

PREP TIME: 3 MINUTES / COOK TIME: 19 MINUTES

Pittas are always encouraged to slow down and enjoy the moment. The preparation of this dosha-balancing rice is the perfect opportunity to be in the moment, relax, and test the idea that a watched pot does indeed boil.

¼ cup coconut oil

5 bay leaves

8 cinnamon sticks

1 teaspoon saffron

2 cups basmati rice

4 cups vegetable broth

1 teaspoon salt

1. In a medium pot over medium heat, heat the coconut oil. Add the bay leaves, cinnamon sticks, and saffron. Cook for 2 to 3 minutes.

2. Add the rice and cook for 2 minutes.

3. Add the broth and salt, and bring to a boil.

4. Reduce the heat to low, cover, and simmer for 15 minutes.

5. Remove the bay leaves and cinnamon sticks and serve.

PITTA

6–8
SERVINGS

SEASON: SUMMER

TASTES: ASTRINGENT, BITTER, PUNGENT, SALTY, SWEET

Vatas *can top with lemon zest and/or a squeeze of lemon juice.*

Pittas *can add cardamom pods and cloves for more cooling.*

Kaphas *can add cayenne for heat and ginger for digestion.*

Timesaving Tip: *Carry a portable charger for your smartphone to keep your cell phone from dying during a hectic day outside the office. While you're commuting, networking, or meeting, your phone can be charging in your handbag or briefcase.*

AFRICAN-SPICED QUINOA WITH PRESERVED LEMON

PREP TIME: 5 MINUTES / COOK TIME: 20 MINUTES

KAPHA

4–6
SERVINGS

SEASON: SPRING

TASTES: ASTRINGENT, BITTER, PUNGENT, SALTY, SOUR, SWEET

Vatas *can add a dollop of yogurt for creaminess.*

Pittas *can omit the paprika and pepper and garnish with freshly chopped cilantro.*

Kaphas *can top with a fried egg.*

Warming African spices combined with sour lemon juices are fantastic balancers for the sweet-craving kapha doshas. This recipe works with a variety of main dishes regardless of their cuisine.

1 tablespoon sunflower oil

2 teaspoons smoked paprika

1 teaspoon freshly ground black pepper

1 teaspoon ground nutmeg

1 teaspoon ground cumin

1 teaspoon ground cinnamon

1 teaspoon ground cloves

2 cups quinoa

3 tablespoons preserved lemon, minced

3 cups vegetable broth

¼ cup freshly squeezed lemon juice

1. In a medium pot, heat the sunflower oil. Add the smoked paprika, black pepper, nutmeg, cumin, cinnamon, and cloves, and cook for 1 minute.

2. Add the quinoa and toast for 2 to 3 minutes.

3. Add the preserved lemon, broth, and lemon juice and bring to a boil.

4. Reduce the heat to low and simmer, covered, for 12 to 15 minutes before serving.

INDIAN-SPICED COUSCOUS WITH CORIANDER

PREP TIME: 3 MINUTES / COOK TIME: 15 MINUTES

Couscous is an incredible balancer for kaphas, vatas, and pittas, but this particular spice blend (warming, spicy) and the use of sunflower oil over ghee lends itself more toward the kapha dosha.

1 tablespoon sunflower oil

1 tablespoon black mustard seeds

2 teaspoons ground cumin

2 teaspoons turmeric

1 teaspoon ground coriander

1 teaspoon fenugreek

5 curry leaves

2 cups Israeli couscous

4½ cups vegetable broth

1. In a medium pot, heat the sunflower oil. Add the mustard seeds, cumin, turmeric, coriander, fenugreek, and curry leaves.

2. Cook for 1 minute, then add the couscous and toast for 2 to 3 minutes.

3. Add the broth, and bring to a boil.

4. Reduce the heat to low and simmer, covered, until the liquid is absorbed, about 10 minutes, and serve.

KAPHA

6–8
SERVINGS

SEASON: WINTER

TASTES: ASTRINGENT, BITTER, PUNGENT, SOUR, SWEET

Vatas *can add a dollop of yogurt for creaminess or a splash of champagne or white balsamic vinegar.*

Pittas *can omit the mustard seeds, curry leaves, and fenugreek and garnish with freshly chopped cilantro or mint.*

Kaphas *can top with a fried egg.*

ROASTED CHICKPEAS WITH SEA SALT

PREP TIME: 10 MINUTES / COOK TIME: 20 MINUTES

PITTA

4–6
SERVINGS

SEASON: SUMMER

TASTES: ASTRINGENT, BITTER, SALTY, SWEET

Vatas *can eat sparingly as a treat or substitute a nut, like cashews or almonds, for the chickpeas.*

Pittas *can halve the sea salt.*

Kaphas *can add ground ginger, cayenne, smoked paprika, and cinnamon for a sweet-spicy taste.*

This recipe is a perfect blank canvas for playing with flavors. While this version is tailored to pittas, more cooling spices, like fennel, cardamom, or cinnamon, make fast, easy, dosha-balancing additions.

2 (15-ounce) cans chickpeas
1 tablespoon sunflower or coconut oil
1 tablespoon turmeric
1 tablespoon sea salt

1. Preheat the oven to 450°F.

2. In a medium bowl, combine the chickpeas, oil, turmeric, and sea salt. Stir so that the spices and oil cover the chickpeas.

3. On a medium pan, spread the chickpeas out and roast for 20 minutes. (These can also be sautéed for 5 to 7 minutes stovetop if outside temps are too high to turn on the oven.)

Mindfulness Tip: *Housework doesn't have to be a dirty word. Turn routine activities you don't love into moving meditation by doing them slowly, deliberately, and mindfully, while noticing each step along the way. Not only will you stay present, but you'll learn to look forward to mundane chores as a mental break.*

CHICKPEAS WITH ARTICHOKES AND FRIED SAGE

PREP TIME: 2 MINUTES / COOK TIME: 10 MINUTES

You'll love the versatility of this side dish, which can stand alone, be served atop your favorite grain, or join with a roundup of interesting mezzes. Enjoy warm or cold, depending on your season and dosha.

¼ cup ghee

1 bunch sage leaves (about 12 to 18)

2 (15-ounce) cans artichoke hearts, drained

2 (15-ounce) cans chickpeas, drained

Squeeze of 1 lemon

1. In a large skillet over medium heat, heat the ghee and add the sage leaves. Cook for 3 to 4 minutes, until crispy.

2. Remove to a plate topped with a paper towel.

3. Add the artichoke hearts and chickpeas to the skillet, and cook for 4 to 5 minutes.

4. Remove the artichoke hearts and chickpeas to a bowl, top with the sage leaves and lemon, and serve.

VATA

4–6
SERVINGS

SEASON: FALL

TASTES: ASTRINGENT, PUNGENT, SOUR, SWEET

Vatas *can switch beans for variety and add smoked paprika or cayenne.*

Pittas *can add more cooling herbs, like fresh basil or dill.*

Kaphas *can add caramelized onions and red chili flakes.*

Ayurvedic Lifestyle Tip: *Switch out your coffee habit for tea, which contains more antioxidants, boosts your immune system, and fights disease. Make your cup even healthier by adding spices like cinnamon or star anise to enhance flavor and nutrients.*

SMASHED BLACK BEANS WITH SMOKED PAPRIKA

PREP TIME: 10 MINUTES

VATA

4–6
SERVINGS

SEASON: FALL

TASTES: ASTRINGENT, BITTER, PUNGENT, SALTY, SOUR, SWEET

Vatas *can switch out beans for variety, add sesame seeds for crunch, or drizzle on some tahini.*

Pittas *can omit or reduce garlic and trade paprika for cumin, thyme, or basil.*

Kaphas *can add lemon zest and red chili flakes.*

This made-in-a-flash side dish is perfect to whip up on a time-crunched weekday night or as a simple snack when guests drop by. Because black beans are tridoshic, you don't have to worry about unbalancing anyone's dosha.

2 (15-ounce) cans black beans, drained
¼ cup freshly squeezed lemon juice
¼ cup olive oil
4 to 6 garlic cloves, minced
3 tablespoons smoked paprika (or more to taste)
¼ teaspoon sea or kosher salt
Chopped scallions, for garnish

1. In a large bowl, smash the black beans with a fork.

2. Stir in the lemon juice, olive oil, garlic, paprika, and salt.

3. Garnish with the scallions and serve.

Timesaving Tip: *When you're ready to get out the door, either in the mornings on your way to work or in the evenings when you're leaving the office, avoid the impulse to squeeze in one more task. One distraction leads to another, which creates stress, disrupts focus, and causes you to be late.*

MEDITERRANEAN WHITE BEANS WITH ROSEMARY

PREP TIME: 10 MINUTES

The key to this simple dish is an abundance of fragrant fresh rosemary, but you can substitute with any herb you find at the farmers' market or in your crisper for a different flavor. It takes minutes to make but pairs well with just about any entrée. Or, serve on top of quinoa for a hearty one-bowl meal.

2 (15-ounce) cans white beans, drained

¼ cup freshly squeezed lemon juice

¼ cup olive oil

4 to 6 garlic cloves, minced

3 tablespoons chopped fresh rosemary

¼ teaspoon sea or kosher salt

Freshly ground black pepper

Toasted pine nuts, for garnish

1. In a large bowl, stir together the white beans, lemon juice, olive oil, garlic, rosemary, and salt.

2. Season with the pepper, top with the pine nuts, and serve.

VATA

4–6
SERVINGS

SEASON: FALL

TASTES: ASTRINGENT, BITTER, PUNGENT, SALTY, SOUR, SWEET

Vatas *can switch out beans for variety and drizzle with olive oil to finish.*

Pittas *can omit or reduce garlic and trade out rosemary for cumin, thyme, or basil.*

Kaphas *can add lemon zest and red chili flakes.*

Mindfulness Tip: *When things don't seem to go your way, remind yourself that the universe works in your favor, not against it, and often what looks less than ideal now works out better in the long run. Look at one thing in your life that gives you joy, and let yourself sit with those happy feelings.*

RED BEANS WITH SESAME AND SCALLIONS

PREP TIME: 10 MINUTES

PITTA

4–6
SERVINGS

SEASON: SUMMER

TASTES: ASTRINGENT, BITTER, PUNGENT, SALTY, SOUR, SWEET

Vatas *can switch out beans for variety and add lemon zest.*

Pittas *can add more cooling herbs, like fresh basil or dill.*

Kaphas *can add lemon zest and red chili flakes.*

Pittas love their summer salads, and this one is bound to make the weekly rotation. It's fast, portable, and flavorful enough to take to a brunch or summer patio party. No one has to know you're balancing their pitta dosha.

2 (15-ounce) cans red or adzuki beans, drained
¼ cup freshly squeezed lemon juice
¼ cup olive oil
1 garlic clove, minced
3 tablespoons toasted sesame seeds (instructions on page 146)
¼ cup chopped scallions
¼ teaspoon sea or kosher salt
Sesame oil, for garnish

1. In a large bowl, stir together the beans, lemon juice, olive oil, garlic, sesame seeds, scallions, and salt.

2. Drizzle with sesame oil and serve.

Ayurvedic Lifestyle Tip: *Aromatherapy is a powerful way to keep calm, stay focused, and enhance positive feelings. Keep a variety of oils at your desk or in your tote to help you stay mindful, creative, and happy when days become hectic or stressful.*

LENTILS WITH SUN-DRIED TOMATOES AND OLIVES

PREP TIME: 5 MINUTES / COOK TIME: 20 MINUTES

Kaphas do well with fruits and vegetables with mildly sweet and sour flavors or cooked with hot spices like pepper, ginger, or garlic. This lentil salad fits the bill, all in under half an hour.

2 cups Le Puy lentils

2 tablespoons turmeric

1 tablespoon sea or kosher salt

¼ cup olive oil

¼ cup tahini

2 tablespoons freshly squeezed lemon juice

1 cup chopped sun-dried tomatoes, drained of oil

¼ cup kalamata olives, chopped

1. In a large saucepan, bring half a pan of water to a boil. Add the lentils and cook until tender, about 15 minutes.

2. Drain and cool.

3. In a medium bowl, whisk together the turmeric, salt, olive oil, tahini, and lemon juice.

4. Add the lentils, sun-dried tomatoes, and olives.

5. Stir to combine and serve.

> Timesaving Tip: *Find yourself at the end of the day with too many unchecked to-dos? Track your time the same way you'd track calories in a diet. Mark down how long it takes you to complete certain tasks (include social media, e-mails, and water-cooler breaks). At the end of two days, go through your tracker and identify the biggest distractions and time wasters.*

KAPHA

4–6
SERVINGS

SEASON: WINTER

TASTES: ASTRINGENT, BITTER, PUNGENT, SALTY, SOUR, SWEET

Vatas *can switch to red lentils and add smoked paprika or cayenne.*

Pittas *can substitute beans or chickpeas for the lentils.*

Kaphas *can add red chili flakes and omit the tahini.*

7

MAIN DISHES

GARLIC AND ONION SPAGHETTI WITH WALNUTS AND SHAVED PARMESAN

PREP TIME: 5 MINUTES / COOK TIME: 20 MINUTES

VATA

2

SERVINGS

SEASON: WINTER

TASTES: ASTRINGENT, BITTER, PUNGENT, SALTY, SOUR, SWEET

Vatas can add a handful of arugula, the zest of the lemon, or more garlic.

Pittas can substitute for the garlic and onion with spinach and mushrooms.

Kaphas can add spinach and chilies, while omitting the Parmesan.

This vata pacifier is about as fast and easy as a dinner recipe can get. Add more dosha balancers, like olives, basil, or fennel, if you've got additional prep time.

4 to 6 ounces dried whole-wheat spaghetti

¼ cup olive oil

4 garlic cloves, minced

1 onion, sliced   + Spinach/

½ cup chopped toasted walnuts   who shroom

2 ounces shaved Parmesan cheese

Squeeze of 1 lemon

Sea salt

Freshly ground black pepper

1. In a large pot of boiling water, cook the spaghetti according to package directions.

2. Drain the pasta, reserving 1 cup of the pasta water.

3. In a large skillet over medium heat, heat the olive oil and sauté the garlic for 1 minute.

4. Add the onion and cook until brown, about 15 minutes.

5. Toss the drained pasta in the skillet with the onion mixture. If you need more "sauce," add a bit of pasta water.

6. Top with the toasted walnuts, Parmesan, lemon, sea salt, and pepper and serve.

> Note: *To toast the walnuts, spread them in an ungreased pan. Bake in an oven preheated to 350°F for 5 to 7 minutes, stirring occasionally, until they begin to brown.*

HERBED SPAGHETTI WITH FRENCH GREEN BEANS

PREP TIME: 5 MINUTES / COOK TIME: 25 MINUTES

If you're balancing pitta energies, serve this chilled or room temp, but kaphas and vatas will want to eat this warm. Of course, the herbs can be mixed and matched with the freshest picks from your market.

4 to 6 ounces dried whole-wheat spaghetti

¼ cup olive oil

2 shallots, minced

2 garlic cloves, minced

4 cups French green beans, trimmed and halved

1 cup chopped fresh basil

1 cup chopped fresh parsley

1 cup chopped fresh mint

1 cup chopped fresh cilantro

Squeeze of 1 lemon

½ cup chopped toasted walnuts (toasting instructions on page 142)

1. In a large pot of boiling water, cook the spaghetti according to the package directions.

2. Drain the pasta, reserving 1 cup of the pasta water.

3. In a large skillet over medium heat, heat the olive oil and sauté the shallots and garlic for 1 minute.

4. Add the beans and cook until al dente, about 3 to 4 minutes.

5. Toss the drained pasta in the skillet with the beans mixture. If you need more "sauce," add a bit of pasta water.

6. Top with the basil, parsley, mint, cilantro, lemon, and walnuts and serve.

PITTA   KAPHA

2–4
SERVINGS

SEASON: SUMMER

TASTES: ASTRINGENT, BITTER, PUNGENT, SALTY, SOUR, SWEET

Vatas *can add a handful of arugula, olives, tomatoes, or more garlic.*

Pittas *can substitute garlic and shallots with spinach and mushrooms.*

Kaphas *can add spinach and chilies.*

BITTERSWEET ARUGULA–POMEGRANATE SPAGHETTI

PREP TIME: 3 MINUTES / COOK TIME: 20 MINUTES

KAPHA

4–6
SERVINGS

SEASONS: LATE WINTER/
EARLY SPRING

TASTES: ASTRINGENT,
BITTER, PUNGENT,
SALTY, SWEET

Vatas can reduce greens
and add chopped pre-
served lemon or onion with
the garlic.

Pittas can omit or reduce
garlic for more support.

Kaphas can add garlic,
onions, and ginger for more
support.

The sweet-spicy combo of peppery greens with sweet pomegranate plays to the kapha and pitta energies. Amp up the flavor profile by adding freshly ground cumin with the garlic or simply adding more garlic.

6 cups arugula
16 ounces dried whole-wheat spaghetti
¼ cup olive oil
3 garlic cloves, minced
2 tablespoons pomegranate molasses
Sea salt
Freshly ground black pepper

1. In a large bowl, place the arugula.

2. In a large pot, cook the spaghetti according to the package directions.

3. In a small skillet over medium heat, heat the oil. Add the garlic and cook for 2 to 3 minutes.

4. Add the pomegranate molasses and heat through.

5. When al dente, drain the pasta, reserving 1 cup of pasta water.

6. Add the hot oil and pasta to the arugula and toss to combine.

7. Add a touch of pasta water if the pasta is too dry.

8. Season with the salt and pepper and serve.

SPICY ASIAN NOODLES WITH ASPARAGUS AND SESAME

PREP TIME: 5 MINUTES / COOK TIME: 20 MINUTES

Pittas don't need extra heat, but sometimes they crave it. This recipe adds a touch of spice and balances it with the rest of the dosha tastes. The toasted nuts and seeds, fresh herbs, and crisp asparagus add textural interest as well as zest.

4 to 6 ounces dried whole-soba, udon, or rice noodles

¼ cup sesame oil

2 garlic cloves, minced

¼ teaspoon red chili flakes

4 cups chopped asparagus

¼ cup soy sauce

¼ cup raw honey

½ cup chopped fresh cilantro

½ cup chopped fresh basil

½ cup chopped toasted peanuts

½ cup toasted sesame seeds

1. In a large pot of boiling water, cook the pasta according to the package directions. Drain.

2. In a large skillet over medium heat, heat the sesame oil. Sauté the garlic and chili flakes for 2 minutes.

3. Add the asparagus and cook until al dente, about 3 to 4 minutes.

4. Add the soy sauce, honey, cilantro, and basil.

RECIPE CONTINUES ON NEXT PAGE

PITTA

2–4
SERVINGS

SEASON: SUMMER

TASTES: ASTRINGENT, BITTER, PUNGENT, SALTY, SOUR, SWEET

Vatas *can double or triple the garlic and add more chili flakes and lemon zest.*

Pittas *can add orange zest to brighten and use less soy sauce.*

Kaphas *can double or triple the garlic, add spinach and chilies, and use less honey.*

5. Toss the drained pasta in the skillet with the oil and spice mixture.

6. Top with the peanuts and sesame seeds, and serve.

Note: *To toast the peanuts, spread them in an ungreased pan. Bake in an oven preheated to 350°F for about 15 minutes, stirring occasionally. To toast the sesame seeds, in a small skillet over medium heat, dry toast them until they brown, about 1 to 2 minutes.*

SPICY-SWEET TOFU BOWL WITH BELL PEPPERS

PREP TIME: 5 MINUTES / COOK TIME: 15 MINUTES

When vatas are feeling restless, worried, or stressed out, this sweet, sour, and salty recipe is a quick fix for the mood. Its flavors are nourishing, nurturing, warm, and grounding.

1 tablespoon coconut oil

1 (1-inch) ginger knob, minced

3 garlic cloves, minced

1 tablespoon turmeric

1 teaspoon sea or kosher salt

1 teaspoon red chili flakes

2 to 3 cups orange, red, or yellow bell peppers, stemmed, seeded, and diced

2 (14-ounce) packages firm tofu, drained and cubed

¾ cup coconut milk

Juice of 1 lemon

1. In a large skillet over medium heat, heat the oil. Add the ginger, garlic, turmeric, salt, and chili flakes.

2. Sauté for 6 to 8 minutes.

3. Add the peppers and tofu, and sauté for 5 minutes.

4. Add the coconut milk and heat through, about 3 minutes.

5. Garnish with the lemon juice and serve.

Mindfulness Tip: *While urgency is critical when you've got a mile-long to-do list, make sure your steps are mindful, focused, and deliberate, which will ensure you do the tasks correctly and enjoy them at the same time.*

VATA

2–4
SERVINGS

SEASONS: FALL/WINTER

TASTES: ASTRINGENT, BITTER, PUNGENT, SALTY, SOUR, SWEET

Vatas *can add a handful of arugula, the zest of the lemon, or more garlic.*

Pittas *can substitute ginger and onion with spinach and mushrooms, and orange or lime juice for the lemon juice.*

Kaphas *can use olive oil for the coconut oil, almond or rice milk for the coconut milk, and chickpeas for the tofu.*

TOFU WITH TOMATOES AND CHILIES

PREP TIME: 5 MINUTES / COOK TIME: 15 MINUTES

VATA

2–4
SERVINGS

SEASONS: FALL/WINTER

TASTES: ASTRINGENT, BITTER, PUNGENT, SALTY, SOUR, SWEET

Vatas *can add a dollop of yogurt or a splash of coconut milk with the tofu.*

Pittas *can substitute the ginger and garlic with spinach and mushrooms, and orange or lime juice for the lemon juice.*

Kaphas *can use olive oil for the coconut oil and chickpeas for the tofu.*

Nourishing and spicy, this dish is the perfect bowl for balancing vata energies. Satisfying alone, it's even better with Stovetop Garlic-Coriander Naan (page 86). Vary the spice and lemon according to your preferences.

1 tablespoon coconut oil
1 (1-inch) ginger knob, minced
3 garlic cloves, minced
2 tablespoons turmeric
2 tablespoons ground cumin
2 tablespoons ground coriander
1 teaspoon sea or kosher salt
2 or 3 Thai chilies
2 (14-ounce) packages firm tofu, drained and cubed
2 to 3 cups chopped heirloom tomatoes
Juice of 1 lemon

1. In a large skillet over medium heat, heat the oil and add the ginger, garlic, turmeric, cumin, coriander, salt, and chilies.

2. Sauté for 6 to 8 minutes.

3. Add the tofu and tomatoes, and sauté for 5 minutes.

4. Garnish with the lemon juice and serve.

> **Ayurvedic Lifestyle Tip:** *Try to sleep by 10 p.m. to give your body the chance to fully experience restorative sleep processes and rejuvenate cells, organs, and systems for the next day. The earlier you fall asleep, the more likely you'll be able to wake up early—another aspect of the Ayurvedic lifestyle.*

TOFU STIR-FRY WITH CURRY LEAVES

PREP TIME: 5 MINUTES, PLUS 10 MINUTES TO MARINATE / COOK TIME: 15 MINUTES

Curry-loving vatas will appreciate the bold curry flavors with a touch of spice. Add more curry leaves to taste for even more intense heat, and be sure to adjust the seasonings to suit your palate.

2 (14-ounce) packages firm tofu, drained and cubed
1 tablespoon paprika
1 tablespoon turmeric
1 tablespoon ground cumin
Juice of 1 lemon
¼ teaspoon salt
1 tablespoon coconut oil
1 (1-inch) ginger knob, minced
3 garlic cloves, minced
5 curry leaves
1 onion, sliced
½ cup toasted shredded coconut (instructions on page 102)

1. In a small bowl, marinate the tofu, paprika, turmeric, cumin, lemon juice, and salt for 10 minutes.

2. In a large skillet over medium heat, heat the oil and add the ginger, garlic, curry leaves, and onion.

3. Sauté for 6 to 8 minutes.

4. Add the marinated tofu with the marinade and cook for 5 minutes.

5. Top with the coconut and serve.

VATA

4–6
SERVINGS

SEASONS: FALL/WINTER

TASTES: ASTRINGENT, BITTER, PUNGENT, SALTY, SOUR, SWEET

Vatas *can add a handful of arugula, a dollop of yogurt, or coconut milk.*

Pittas *can substitute the ginger, curry, and onion with spinach and mushrooms.*

Kaphas *can use chickpeas instead of the tofu.*

CHERRY-ALMOND COUSCOUS WITH TOFU AND GREENS

PREP TIME: 10 MINUTES / COOK TIME: 15 MINUTES

PITTA

6—8
SERVINGS

SEASON: SUMMER

TASTES: ASTRINGENT, BITTER, PUNGENT, SALTY, SOUR, SWEET

Vatas *can add a dollop of yogurt for creaminess or a splash of champagne or white balsamic vinegar. Steam the raw greens and tofu before serving.*

Pittas *can garnish with freshly chopped cilantro or mint.*

Kaphas *can top with a fried egg, use chickpeas instead of tofu, use almond milk instead of coconut milk, and use sunflower oil instead of coconut oil.*

A light, airy, refreshing salad is the perfect counterpart to the pitta energies, which run on the hot side. Serve chilled or room temperature. Kaphas and vatas can also sauté the tofu if they have time.

1 tablespoon coconut, almond, or olive oil
1 cup chopped almonds
1 cup chopped ripe cherries
2 cups Israeli couscous
4½ cups vegetable broth
½ cup coconut milk
1 tablespoon freshly squeezed lemon juice
1 tablespoon ground fennel
1 tablespoon ground cardamom
Pinch of salt
½ cup dried cherries
½ cup slivered almonds
2 (14-ounce) packages tofu, drained and cubed
6 to 8 cups salad greens

1. In a large pot, heat the oil. Add the almonds and cherries, and cook for 1 minute.

2. Add the couscous, and toast for 2 to 3 minutes.

3. Add the broth, bring to a boil, reduce the heat to low, and simmer, covered, until the liquid is absorbed, about 10 minutes.

4. In a large bowl, whisk the coconut milk, lemon juice, fennel, cardamom, and salt.

5. Add in the couscous, dried cherries, almonds, and tofu, and stir to combine.

6. Serve the mixture over the salad greens.

THAI BASIL TOFU BOWL WITH QUINOA

PREP TIME: 8 MINUTES / COOK TIME: 22 MINUTES

This healthy vegetarian spin on take-out Thai basil chicken beautifully balances the pitta energies in the summer thanks to coconut, mint, and basil. Serve with chapati or naan and chutney.

1 (14-ounce) package firm tofu, drained and cubed

½ cup soy sauce

1 tablespoon coconut oil

1 teaspoon minced fresh ginger

1 (15-ounce) can coconut milk

1 cup quinoa

1 bunch fresh basil or Thai basil, chopped

1 cup chopped toasted sunflower seeds

¼ cup fresh mint, chopped

½ cup toasted shredded coconut (instructions on page 102)

1. In a small bowl, stir together the tofu and soy sauce.

2. In a large skillet, heat the oil. Add the ginger, and sauté for 2 minutes.

3. Add the tofu, and sauté until brown, about 5 to 6 minutes.

4. Reduce the heat to low and add the coconut milk, quinoa, and basil. Cook for 15 minutes.

5. Garnish with the sunflower seeds, mint, and coconut.

Note: *To toast the sunflower seeds, in a small skillet over medium heat, dry toast them until they brown, about 2 to 3 minutes.*

PITTA

4–6
SERVINGS

SEASON: SUMMER

TASTES: ASTRINGENT, BITTER, PUNGENT, SALTY, SWEET

Vatas *can add freshly ground black pepper, cayenne, or red chili flakes to the tofu. Fresh garlic and onions work well, too.*

Pittas *can add fresh spinach or chopped kale.*

Kaphas *can use sunflower oil rather than coconut oil and add freshly ground black pepper, cayenne, or red chili flakes to the tofu. Fresh garlic and onions work well, too.*

TOFU AND BROCCOLI STIR-FRY

PREP TIME: 5 MINUTES / COOK TIME: 10 MINUTES

PITTA

2–4
SERVINGS

SEASON: SUMMER

TASTES: ASTRINGENT,
BITTER, PUNGENT, SALTY,
SOUR, SWEET

Vatas *can add black pepper, cayenne, vinegar, or chili sauce to the tofu. Substitute green beans or asparagus for the broccoli.*

Pittas *can add fresh spinach or snow peas and halve or omit the ginger.*

Kaphas *can use chickpeas instead of tofu and sunflower oil rather than coconut oil and add freshly ground black pepper, cayenne, or red chili flakes. Fresh garlic and onions work well, too.*

You'll love that this recipe can be served hot or cold, depending on the season and your dosha. Pittas prefer this room temp or chilled, while kaphas and vatas can serve it straight from the stove.

1 (14-ounce) package firm tofu, drained and cubed
½ cup soy sauce
1 tablespoon coconut oil
1 teaspoon minced fresh ginger
2 cups broccoli florets (can use prepackaged)
1 bunch fresh basil or Thai basil, chopped
½ cup toasted sesame seeds (instructions on page 146)
1 cup chopped tomatoes

1. In a small bowl, stir together the tofu and the soy sauce.

2. In a large skillet over medium heat, heat the oil. Add the ginger, and sauté for 2 minutes.

3. Add the broccoli and tofu, and sauté for 5 minutes.

4. Reduce the heat to low and add the basil. Cook for 1 to 2 minutes, or until the basil wilts.

5. Garnish with the sesame seeds and tomatoes.

6. Serve alone or with quinoa, rice, or chapati.

Timesaving Tip: *You don't have to skip the frozen food section anymore. Despite the bad reputation (and one that's often well-deserved) of TV dinners and other frozen meals, frozen organic vegetables can be your best bet, especially when buying produce that's out of season.*

TOFU AND SWISS CHARD WITH PUMPKIN SEEDS

PREP TIME: 5 MINUTES / COOK TIME: 10 MINUTES

This simple stir-fry can be made creamier and more indulgent with a dollop of yogurt, which falls into the sour and sweet taste categories. Add more nutrients by tossing in fresh herbs and vegetables.

3 tablespoons coconut oil

3 shallots, minced

2 garlic cloves, minced

1 tablespoon mild curry powder

1 (14-ounce) package firm tofu, drained and cubed

3 cups stemmed and chopped Swiss chard

½ cup toasted pumpkin seeds

Splash of vinegar or squeeze of 1 lemon

1. In a large skillet over medium heat, heat the oil. Add the shallots, garlic, and curry powder, and sauté for 2 minutes.

2. Add the tofu, and cook for 4 to 5 minutes.

3. Toss in the chard and cook for 3 to 5 minutes.

4. Top with the pumpkin seeds and lemon juice.

5. Serve with quinoa, rice, or chapati.

Note: *To toast the pumpkin seeds, spread them in a pan, drizzle with olive or coconut oil, and stir to coat. Bake them in an oven preheated to 350°F for 5 to 15 minutes, depending on seed size, stirring occasionally, until golden brown.*

VATA

2–4
SERVINGS

SEASON: SUMMER

TASTES: ASTRINGENT, BITTER, PUNGENT, SALTY, SOUR, SWEET

Vatas *can add freshly ground black pepper, cayenne, or chili sauce to the tofu. Substitute green beans or asparagus for the chard.*

Pittas *can halve or omit the shallots and/or substitute fennel. Garnish with fresh mint.*

Kaphas *can use chickpeas instead of tofu and sunflower oil rather than coconut oil and add freshly ground black pepper, cayenne, or red chili flakes. Fresh garlic and onions work well, too.*

CHICKPEAS AND POTATOES WITH TAMARIND

PREP TIME: 5 MINUTES / COOK TIME: 25 MINUTES

KAPHA

6–8
SERVINGS

SEASONS: LATE WINTER/ SPRING

TASTES: ASTRINGENT, BITTER, PUNGENT, SALTY, SOUR, SWEET

Vatas can omit the fenugreek and use olive oil, coconut oil, or ghee instead of the sunflower oil.

Pittas can halve or omit the chili powder, onions, ginger, and chilies.

Kaphas can add more spices or tamarind, plus a dollop of raw honey for more sweet.

This hearty bowl of nutritious comfort is an excellent pacifier of pitta energies. It has a fiery bite that gets you up and moving.

3 potatoes, cubed
¼ cup sunflower oil
2 tablespoons turmeric
2 tablespoons cumin seeds
2 tablespoons ground coriander
1 tablespoon fenugreek
1 tablespoon chili powder
2 onions, chopped
1 (1-inch) ginger knob, minced
2 to 3 Thai chilies
2 to 3 tablespoons tamarind paste
2 (15-ounce) cans chickpeas, drained
¾ cup chopped fresh cilantro
¾ cup chopped fresh mint
Squeeze of 1 lemon

1. In a large saucepan over high heat, boil the potatoes for 5 to 6 minutes. Drain.

2. In a large skillet, heat the oil and add the turmeric, cumin, coriander, fenugreek, and chili powder.

3. Cook for 1 minute.

4. Add the onions, ginger, chilies, tamarind, and potatoes, and cook for 8 to 10 minutes.

5. Add the chickpeas to the skillet, and cook for 4 to 5 minutes.

6. Top with the cilantro, mint, and lemon juice.

7. Serve with basmati rice, quinoa, naan, or chapati and tamarind chutney.

CURRIED CHICKPEAS WITH CILANTRO

PREP TIME: 5 MINUTES / COOK TIME: 15 MINUTES

This versatile recipe can be served as a side dish or an entrée. Fresh greens are an excellent addition, and kaphas with a sweet tooth can add a touch of raw honey to soothe any cravings.

¼ cup ghee

2 tablespoons turmeric

2 tablespoons cumin seeds

2 tablespoons ground coriander

1 tablespoon fenugreek

1 tablespoon garam masala

2 onions, chopped

1 (1-inch) ginger knob, minced

2 (15-ounce) cans chickpeas, drained

1 cup water, divided

¾ cup chopped fresh cilantro

Squeeze of 1 lemon

1. In a large skillet, heat the ghee. Add the turmeric, cumin, coriander, fenugreek, and garam masala, and cook for 1 minute.

2. Add the onions and ginger, and cook for 8 to 10 minutes.

3. Add the chickpeas to the skillet. Cook for 4 to 5 minutes, then stir in the water in ¼ cup increments to create a sauce.

4. Top with the cilantro and lemon.

5. Serve with basmati rice, quinoa, naan, or chapati.

KAPHA

2–4
SERVINGS

SEASON: SUMMER

TASTES: ASTRINGENT, BITTER, PUNGENT, SALTY, SOUR, SWEET

Vatas *can add garlic or use coconut milk instead of water and omit the fenugreek.*

Pittas *can use coconut oil instead of ghee.*

Kaphas *can add spinach and chilies.*

1ATAR PANEER

15 MINUTES

wist on traditional matar paneer uses a healthy array of
nd ground spices to maximize healing and dosha tastes.

·aw cashews
;poons ghee
2 large onions, sliced
¼ cup minced fresh ginger
1 tablespoon red chili powder
2 tablespoons ground coriander
1 tablespoon ground cumin
1 tablespoon turmeric
2 cups chopped tomatoes
1 tablespoon tomato paste
1 tablespoon ghee or olive oil
2 cups cubed paneer (packaged is fine)
1 cup fresh or frozen green peas
1 tablespoon garam masala
1 to 2 tablespoons coconut milk

1. Soak cashews in hot water (enough to cover) for 10 minutes, then grind to a paste.

2. In a large skillet over medium heat, heat the ghee and add the onions and ginger, and sauté for 2 minutes.

3. Add the chili powder, coriander, cumin, and turmeric. Saute 1 minute, then add the tomatoes and tomato paste. Cook 5 minutes.

4. Meanwhile, in a separate skillet over medium-high heat, sauté the oil and paneer until brown on both sides, about 3 to 4 minutes, then set aside.

5. Heat through, about 2 minutes, then stir in the garam masala and coconut milk.

Vatas *can add red chilies for spice.*

Pittas *can lessen or omit the chili powder and ginger and halve the onions and garlic. Garnish with mint to cool.*

Kaphas *can use almond milk instead of the coconut milk. Garnish with mint for sweetness.*

SPICY COCONUT LENTILS WITH MINT

PREP TIME: 5 MINUTES / COOK TIME: 22 MINUTES

Spicy Middle Eastern-inspired foods are the perfect energy-balancing comfort foods when vatas feel imbalanced. The roundup of spices ensures you hit all the Ayurvedic tastes. Add raisins, figs, or apricots for more Middle Eastern flair.

2 cups canned or fresh lentils

1 (14-ounce) can coconut milk

3 tablespoons minced fresh ginger

3 tablespoons olive oil

1 tablespoon ground chili powder

1 tablespoon cumin seeds

1 tablespoon turmeric

4 garlic cloves, minced

2 large onions, sliced

½ cup toasted coconut flakes (instructions on page 102)

Juice of 1 lime

1 cup chopped fresh mint

1 cup toasted cashews (follow peanut-toasting instructions on page 146)

1. In a large saucepan over medium heat, cook the lentils with the coconut milk and ginger for 10 minutes.

2. In a large skillet over medium heat, heat the olive oil and add the chili powder, cumin seeds, and turmeric. Cook for 1 minute.

3. Add the garlic and onions, and cook for 10 minutes.

4. Add the lentils and their broth to the spice mixture.

5. Top with the coconut flakes, lime juice, mint, and cashews.

VATA

4–6
SERVINGS

SEASONS: FALL/WINTER

TASTES: ASTRINGENT, BITTER, PUNGENT, SALTY, SOUR, SWEET

Vatas *can add a dollop of yogurt or lemon zest plus chopped fresh figs or dried apricots.*

Pittas *can lessen or omit the chili powder and ginger and halve the onions and garlic.*

Kaphas *can substitute water for half of the coconut milk or use almond milk instead of the coconut milk.*

8

DELIGHTFUL DESSERTS

MINTY PEACH COMPOTE

PREP TIME: 2 MINUTES / COOK TIME: 20 MINUTES

VATA

6–8
SERVINGS

SEASONS: FALL/WINTER

TASTES: ASTRINGENT,
PUNGENT, SOUR, SWEET

Vatas *can also use apricots
and a pinch of sea salt.*

Pittas *can substitute cherries
or figs for the peaches.*

Kaphas *can add some ginger
or lemon zest.*

This fantastic roundup of warm spices is reminiscent of the holiday season. Feel free to spike it with some chilies, fresh ginger, or freshly ground black pepper for more heat and pungency.

½ cup water
¼ cup ghee
3 cinnamon sticks
6 cloves
8 allspice berries
1 pound peaches, pitted and halved
1 cup fresh mint leaves

1. In a large saucepan, bring the water, ghee, cinnamon, cloves, and allspice to a boil.

2. Reduce the heat and simmer for 5 to 10 minutes.

3. Stir in the peaches, cover, and let rest for 10 to 15 minutes.

4. Remove the cinnamon sticks, garnish with the mint, and serve.

Mindfulness Tip: *Worried? Stressed out? Focus on someone else instead. Give a coworker a compliment, thank your barista for an amazing cup of coffee, or tell someone you love how much they mean to you. Turning yourself outward and expressing positive emotions allows others to return those feelings back to you.*

BROWN SUGAR POACHED PEARS WITH ORANGE ZEST

PREP TIME: 5 MINUTES / COOK TIME: 20 MINUTES

Kaphas may want to watch their brown sugar content on this and err on the side of the raw honey, which is more pacifying, if they're feeling imbalanced.

6 pears, peeled, halved, and pitted

2 cups plus 1 tablespoon orange juice, divided

1 cup almond milk

¼ cup raw honey

¼ cup brown sugar

1 tablespoon vanilla extract

1 teaspoon ground ginger

¼ cup orange zest

1. In a large saucepan over medium heat, heat the pears, 2 cups of orange juice, almond milk, honey, and brown sugar until simmering.

2. Add the vanilla, ginger, orange zest, and remaining 1 tablespoon of orange juice.

3. Cover and simmer for 15 minutes. Serve.

KAPHA

SERVINGS

SEASON: WINTER

TASTES: ASTRINGENT, PUNGENT, SALTY, SOUR, SWEET

Vatas *can also use apricots and a pinch of sea salt.*

Pittas *can substitute cherries or figs for the peaches, omit the ginger, and garnish or boil with a touch of saffron.*

Kaphas *can add warming spices like nutmeg, cinnamon sticks, or allspice.*

Ayurvedic Lifestyle Tip: *Need a snack? Rather than an oily, fried, or processed snack from a vending machine or bodega, stick to fresh whole fruits or fruit juices to satisfy your hunger between meals.*

SAFFRON CARROT HALWA WITH PISTACHIOS

PREP TIME: 5 MINUTES / COOK TIME: 25 MINUTES

KAPHA

6–8
SERVINGS

SEASON: SUMMER

TASTES: ASTRINGENT, BITTER, PUNGENT, SALTY, SWEET

Vatas *can use coconut milk for almond milk and add a pinch of sea salt.*

Pittas *can substitute cherries or figs for the carrots and use coconut milk for almond milk.*

Kaphas *can add warming spices like nutmeg, cinnamon sticks, or allspice.*

This twist on the traditional carrot halwa recipe can be riffed on to suit to your tastes with almost any fruit. Almonds or walnuts are also a fantastic substitute for pistachios.

¼ cup sunflower oil

2½ pounds carrots, grated (can use prepackaged)

21 ounces almond milk

12 green cardamom pods, bruised

1 cup chopped pistachios

1 to 2 tablespoons saffron

½ cup raw honey or maple syrup

1. In a large saucepan over medium heat, heat the oil, add the carrots, and cook for 10 minutes.

2. In a small saucepan over medium heat, bring the almond milk, cardamom, pistachios, and saffron to a boil. Reduce to simmer, then cover and set aside until the carrots are cooked to desired doneness, about 5 minutes.

3. Add the almond-saffron milk and cardamom to the carrots and simmer for 10 minutes.

4. Stir in the honey and serve.

> Timesaving Tip: *Reward yourself for jobs well done. Whether you're completing a task you dread or find yourself leaving the house in the morning early, give yourself a little treat, something as small as praise to as large as that new yoga tank you've been eyeing. Incentives can help keep you motivated and on task.*

CACAO DATE BALLS

PREP TIME: 5 MINUTES / COOK TIME: 10 MINUTES

These amazing balls of wonder don't have to wait for dessert. Serve them midday with a cup of tea as a pick-me-up in lieu of that bag of chips from the vending machine. Your body and your taste buds will thank you.

2 cups dates, pitted

2 cups almonds

1 cup cacao nibs

1 tablespoon ground cinnamon

1 teaspoon vanilla extract

Coconut oil, for blending (if needed)

Almond or coconut flour, for blending (if needed)

½ cup cacao powder

1. In a medium saucepan over medium heat, boil the dates until soft, about 5 to 8 minutes. Set aside to cool.

2. In a blender or food processor, blend the almonds, cacao nibs, cinnamon, and vanilla until well blended.

3. Add the dates, and blend again.

4. Add the coconut oil if the mixture is too dry. If it's too wet or sticky, add the almond flour.

5. Roll into balls, coat or dust with the cacao powder, and serve.

PITTA

SERVING SIZE VARIES DEPENDING ON SIZE OF BALLS

SEASON: SUMMER

TASTES: ASTRINGENT, BITTER, PUNGENT, SWEET

Vatas *can sprinkle with sea salt and toasted coconut.*

Pittas *can sprinkle with toasted coconut.*

Kaphas *can substitute figs in place of the dates.*

Mindfulness Tip: *Spend time with someone you love, whether it's your best friend, a family member, or a new acquaintance you'd like to know better, and relish your time together. This will take your mind off preoccupations and immerse you in what you enjoy.*

CHEWY COCONUT BALLS WITH PEPITAS

PREP TIME: 7 MINUTES

PITTA

12–15
BALLS

SEASON: SUMMER

TASTES: ASTRINGENT, BITTER, PUNGENT, SALTY, SWEET

Vatas *can garnish with sea salt and toasted coconut.*

Pittas *can coat with cacao powder and orange zest.*

Kaphas *can add a pinch of cayenne or ground ginger and garnish with orange zest.*

These one-bite wonders are literally bursting with energy. They make a fantastic pack-along snack or a nutritious breakfast on the go—if you actually have leftovers after dessert.

½ cup pumpkin seeds
1 cup shredded toasted coconut (instructions on page 102)
2 tablespoons chia seeds
½ tablespoon ground cardamom
½ tablespoon ground cinnamon
1 tablespoon raw honey or molasses
¼ teaspoon salt
¼ cup coconut oil
Toasted pumpkin seeds (pepitas), for garnish
    (instructions on page 153)

1. In a blender, blend the pumpkin seeds, coconut, chia seeds, cardamom, cinnamon, honey, salt, and coconut oil.

2. Roll into balls and coat or dust in pepitas.

3. Refrigerate until ready to eat.

> **Ayurvedic Lifestyle Tip:** *Ayurveda is all about achieving balance and avoiding extremes, which is especially true when it comes to temperatures. Avoid extremely hot or cold temperatures in your surroundings—say a very hot bath or running outside in the cold—and in your foods. Steer clear of scalding hot coffees, soups, or stews, and avoid ultracold smoothies, ice creams, and drinks.*

BANANA "ICE CREAM" WITH ALMONDS

PREP TIME: 3 MINUTES

Try this faux ice cream when you want to feel like you're being indulgent, but your waistline or your dosha can't afford to. Top with cacao nibs or cacao powder to tame the summer sweet tooth.

6 frozen bananas
1 cup chopped almonds

1. In a food processor or blender, add the bananas and whip until smooth.
2. Top with the almonds and serve.

PITTA

4–6

SERVINGS

SEASON: SUMMER

TASTES: ASTRINGENT, BITTER, SWEET

Vatas *can sprinkle with sea salt and toasted coconut.*
Pittas *can replace the bananas with mangoes.*
Kaphas *can replace the bananas with peaches.*

Timesaving Tip: *Install drawer dividers for everything from underwear and socks to T-shirts, shorts, and workout wear. Keeping clothes folded and separated gives you more space, plus it reduces the time you'll spend digging around for your favorite yoga pants.*

NUTTY BLUEBERRY FIG ICE CREAM

PREP TIME: 5 MINUTES

VATA

2–4
SERVINGS

SEASON: SUMMER

TASTES: ASTRINGENT,
BITTER, SOUR, SALTY, SWEET

Vatas *can sprinkle with sea salt and toasted coconut.*

Pittas *can substitute the blueberries with cherries.*

Kaphas *can sprinkle with chopped fresh mint or basil.*

Turn this faux ice cream into a power shake by adding some almond milk and protein powder; otherwise, reserve it for a dosha-balancing after-dinner treat, sans the fat and calories.

1 cup frozen blueberries
2 cups figs (fresh or frozen)
½ cup almond butter (or 1 cup almonds)
½ cup chopped almonds

1. In a food processor or blender, whip the blueberries until smooth.

2. Add the figs and almond butter and blend until smooth. If the mixture is too chunky, add a tablespoon of water.

3. Top with the almonds and serve.

Mindfulness Tip: *Distractions at work and home aren't uncommon, but they don't have to stress you out. Instead of trying to beat them, join them! Tune into the sounds around you—a noisy printer, coworker chitchat, a lawn mower outside, or ambient music—and let them bring you to the present moment. Notice how you feel when you hear them, and let those feelings go.*

SAFFRON VANILLA CHIA PUDDING

PREP TIME: 25 MINUTES

Vata, pitta, and kapha alike can enjoy the tridoshic and nutritious chia seed. Here, they're sweetened with bananas, vanilla, and coconut milk and spiced up with saffron and cinnamon.

½ cup chia seeds

2 cups coconut or almond milk

2 mashed bananas

3 tablespoons vanilla extract

1 teaspoon saffron

¼ teaspoon ground cinnamon

1. In a medium bowl, stir together the chia seeds and coconut milk.

2. Set aside for 20 minutes.

3. Add the bananas, vanilla, saffron, and cinnamon.

4. Mix well and serve.

VATA PITTA

2

SERVINGS

SEASON: SUMMER

TASTES: ASTRINGENT, BITTER, PUNGENT, SWEET

Vatas *can sprinkle with sea salt and toasted coconut.*

Pittas *can add chopped fresh basil or mint to garnish.*

Kaphas *can substitute cherries or figs for the bananas.*

Ayurvedic Lifestyle Tip: *Ayurveda wants you to surround yourself in nature. Pets count as nature! Take your dog for long walks, spend time with your cat, or let the peaceful environment of your fish tank become a meditation. Both you and your four-legged or finned friends will benefit.*

WILD BERRY CHOCOLATE CHIA PUDDING

PREP TIME: 25 MINUTES

KAPHA

2
SERVINGS

SEASON: WINTER

TASTES: ASTRINGENT, BITTER, PUNGENT, SOUR, SWEET

Vatas *can sprinkle with sea salt and toasted coconut.*

Pittas *can use coconut milk and add chopped fresh basil or mint to garnish.*

Kaphas *can add orange zest.*

Berries add a sweet and sour flavor to this chia pudding. This dessert is a good choice to serve no matter who's around, as chia seeds are one thing all three doshas are able to agree on.

½ cup chia seeds

2 cups almond milk

1 to 2 cups berries of choice (strawberries, cherries, blueberries)

¼ cup cacao powder or nibs

2 tablespoons raw honey

½ cup slivered toasted almonds (follow walnut-toasting instructions on page 142)

1. In a medium bowl, stir together the chia seeds and almond milk.

2. Set aside for 20 minutes.

3. Add the berries, cacao powder, honey, and almonds.

4. Mix well and serve.

Timesaving Tip: *Create a running shopping list in the notes section of your smart phone or on a sheet of paper posted in your kitchen or office. When items run low, you and/or your family members can update the list in real time, which means spending less time later trying to track down what you need before shopping. Rule is: last one to use, writes it on the list.*

ALMOND–CHOCOLATE AVOCADO PUDDING

PREP TIME: 10 MINUTES

The only thing that can make this soothing, rich pudding more pitta-pacifying is to stick it in the fridge for 20 minutes before serving. Pittas, like their food, are easier to handle when they're chilled out.

2 avocados, peeled and pitted
¼ cup raw honey or molasses
¼ cup cacao nibs or powder
⅓ to ½ cup almond milk
1 tablespoon vanilla extract
½ teaspoon ground cardamom
½ teaspoon ground cinnamon
½ cup shredded toasted coconut (instructions on page 102)

1. In a blender, blend the avocados, honey, cacao nibs, almond milk, vanilla, cardamom, and cinnamon until smooth.

2. Top with the coconut and serve.

PITTA

2–4
SERVINGS

SEASON: SUMMER

TASTES: BITTER, SWEET

Vatas *can add ginger and sprinkle with sea salt.*

Pittas *can use coconut milk instead of almond and add chopped fresh basil or mint to garnish.*

Kaphas *can substitute figs, peaches, mangoes, or apricots for the avocado.*

Mindfulness Tip: *Mentally commit to staying present all day. Before you start your morning, set the intention that you will stay focused, in the moment, and emotionally grounded no matter what life throws at you today. Reminding yourself of your intention throughout the day easily brings your mind to the present.*

LEFTOVER BASMATI RICE PUDDING WITH CINNAMON, ORANGE ZEST, AND VANILLA

PREP TIME: 3 MINUTES

PITTA   KAPHA

2
SERVINGS

SEASONS: SUMMER/SPRING

TASTES: ASTRINGENT, BITTER, PUNGENT, SOUR, SWEET

Vatas *can substitute pineapples for the pears or sprinkle with sea salt and toasted coconut.*

Pittas *can use coconut milk instead of almond and add chopped fresh basil or mint to garnish.*

Kaphas *can add orange zest.*

Most people consider leftover rice destined for frying, but why not dessert instead? This quick rice pudding can also make use of whatever fruits are ripe and ready to eat in your crisper.

1 cup leftover cooked basmati rice
1 cup almond milk
Peels of 1 to 2 oranges
1 to 2 vanilla beans, split lengthwise
2 tablespoons cinnamon (ground or freshly grated toasted sticks)

1. In a medium bowl, stir together the rice and almond milk.

2. Serve garnished with the orange peels, vanilla beans, and cinnamon.

Ayurvedic Lifestyle Tip: *Surround yourself with happy people in order to maintain a peaceful, balanced life. The more drama, negativity, or stress in your life, the more your health is compromised. Choose friends who uplift you and add positive experiences to your world.*

ALMOND PUMPKIN PUDDING

PREP TIME: 25 MINUTES

The taste and texture of this amazing pudding will have you wondering how it can possibly be healthy, but it is. Pittas can chill this overnight and serve cold.

1 (14-ounce) can pumpkin purée

2 cups almond or coconut milk

¼ cup chia seeds

1 cup chopped figs or dates

¼ cup almond butter

1 tablespoon vanilla extract

1 tablespoon raw honey

1 teaspoon ground allspice

1 teaspoon ground ginger

1 teaspoon ground cloves

¼ teaspoon sea or kosher salt

1. In a blender or bowl, blend or mix the pumpkin, almond milk, chia seeds, figs, almond butter, vanilla, honey, allspice, ginger, cloves, and salt until well incorporated.

2. Chill for 20 minutes to set.

3. Serve.

Timesaving Tip: *Plan menus in advance, and if possible, use the same menu lineups twice in the same month. This streamlines grocery shopping and shaves time off of thinking about what you need to prepare and shop for midweek.*

VATA

2–4
SERVINGS

SEASONS: FALL/WINTER

TASTES: ASTRINGENT, BITTER, PUNGENT, SALTY, SOUR, SWEET

Vatas *can garnish with sea salt and toasted coconut.*

Pittas *can garnish with pumpkin seeds and orange zest.*

Kaphas *can add orange zest and sunflower seeds to garnish.*

9

CHUTNEYS, SAUCES, AND DRESSINGS

CARROT-BEET RAITA WITH FENNEL

PREP TIME: 10 MINUTES

VATA

6–8
SERVINGS

SEASON: FALL

TASTES: ASTRINGENT, BITTER, PUNGENT, SALTY, SOUR, SWEET

Vatas can add a grind of black pepper.

Pittas can substitute cucumber for the carrot and garnish with orange zest.

Kaphas can use soy yogurt.

This recipe is well balanced in taste, leaning toward the vata-balancing ingredients. Adding a pinch of spices is the easiest way to adjust this staple to your dosha.

2 cups plain Greek or regular yogurt
½ cup shredded carrot (can use prepackaged)
½ cup shredded beets
½ cup shredded fennel
Pinch of sea or kosher salt
¼ teaspoon ground coriander or fenugreek
2 tablespoons chopped fennel fronds (optional)

1. In a medium bowl, combine the yogurt, carrot, beets, fennel, salt, and coriander.

2. Mix well, adding a tablespoon of water if the mixture is too thick.

3. Garnish with the fennel fronds (if using) and serve.

Mindfulness Tip: *If you're experiencing negative emotions, like stress, anger, or fear, move those feelings through your body without holding onto them. The more you focus on the emotions, the more you experience them. But when you acknowledge you're feeling a certain way and let it move on, you more quickly get back to feeling normal.*

CILANTRO–RADISH RAITA

PREP TIME: 6 MINUTES

Cilantro is tridoshic, so feel free to bulk up this herb regardless of your dosha type. This recipe goes well with curries but doubles as a refreshing dip with fruit slices.

2 cups plain Greek or regular yogurt
¾ cup shredded carrot (can use prepackaged)
¾ cup shredded radish
¾ cup chopped fresh cilantro
¼ teaspoon ground turmeric
Pinch of ground cinnamon
Pinch of sea or kosher salt
1 to 2 tablespoons chopped fennel fronds

1. In a medium bowl, combine the yogurt, carrot, radish, cilantro, turmeric, cinnamon, and salt.

2. Mix well, adding a tablespoon of water if the mixture is too thick.

3. Garnish with the fennel fronds and serve.

PITTA

6–8
SERVINGS

SEASON: SUMMER

TASTES: ASTRINGENT, BITTER, PUNGENT, SALTY, SOUR, SWEET

Vatas *can add a grind of black pepper and lemon zest.*

Pittas *can garnish with lime or orange zest.*

Kaphas *can use soy yogurt.*

Ayurvedic Lifestyle Tip: *Ghee, or clarified butter, isn't part of fad diets, but it's a key component to Ayurveda meals. Use in place of cooking oils—you'll need half as much—to bring out the nutrients in spices, herbs, and vegetables; aid in digestion; and reduce the acidity in your meals.*

DATE AND GINGER CHUTNEY

PREP TIME: 5 MINUTES

VATA

6—8
SERVINGS

SEASON: FALL

TASTES: PUNGENT, SALTY,
SOUR, SWEET

Vatas *can add a grind of black pepper, a pinch of cayenne, and lemon zest.*

Pittas *can garnish with lime or orange zest.*

Kaphas *can add use lime juice instead of orange juice, which lessens the sweetness.*

This recipe falls into the tridoshic category, although it can be a touch sweet for kaphas and a tad spicy for pittas. If you're feeling imbalanced, adjust the citrus and ginger, respectively.

2 cups fresh dates, pitted
¼ cup fresh ginger
1 to 2 tablespoons orange juice
1 teaspoon sea or kosher salt

1. In a blender, blend the dates, ginger, orange juice, and salt.

2. If the consistency is too thick, add more juice or a touch of water.

Timesaving Tip: *Prep food as you unpack your groceries. Wash and chop produce, and separate into servings. By taking the extra time to prep food before you need it, you have it ready to go when it's time to cook.*

APPLE CHUTNEY WITH MUSTARD SEEDS AND STAR ANISE

PREP TIME: 3 MINUTES / COOK TIME: 26 MINUTES

This sweet-savory chutney pairs perfectly with baked goods, as well as the naans, kitcharis, and other meals listed in this book. Add a splash of balsamic vinegar for depth.

2 tablespoons sunflower oil or ghee

2 large onions, chopped

2 tablespoons minced mustard seeds

1 tablespoon minced ginger

½ teaspoon ground allspice

3 to 4 star anise

1 or 2 dried red chili peppers

2 large apples, chopped

1 teaspoon sea or kosher salt

1. In a skillet over medium heat, heat the oil. Add the onions, and cook for 5 minutes.

2. Add the mustard seeds and ginger, cook another minute.

3. Stir in the allspice, star anise, chilies, apples, and salt. Cook 20 minutes.

4. Serve.

VATA KAPHA

6–8
SERVINGS

SEASONS: WINTER/SPRING

TASTES: ASTRINGENT, BITTER, PUNGENT, SALTY, SOUR, SWEET

Vatas *can add coconut powder or ginger for more support.*

Pittas *can halve the onions or omit the ginger and add turmeric, coriander, and cardamom.*

Kaphas *can add fenugreek or turmeric.*

> **Mindfulness Tip:** *Know that saying, "keep your eye on the prize?" To stay mindful, keep your eye on the steps along the way instead. When you focus on what you love doing rather than the success you'll achieve when you get there, you're more likely to reach your goal sooner and with more joy.*

SAVORY ONION–TOMATO CHUTNEY

PREP TIME: 5 MINUTES

KAPHA

6–8
SERVINGS

SEASONS: WINTER/SPRING

TASTES: ASTRINGENT, BITTER, PUNGENT, SALTY, SOUR, SWEET

Vatas can add additional mustard seed, coconut powder, or ginger for more support.

Pittas can halve the onions or omit the ginger and add turmeric, coriander, and cardamom.

Kaphas can add fenugreek or turmeric.

This savory chutney is the ideal partner for many of the kitcharis listed in the book as well as a simple spread for the baked goods, especially those that tend to be sweeter.

2 tablespoons sunflower oil or ghee

2 tablespoons minced fresh ginger

1 or 2 dried red chili peppers

2 large ripe tomatoes, chopped

2 large onions, chopped

¼ cup shredded coconut

1 tablespoon mustard seeds

1 tablespoon urad dal

2 curry leaves

1 teaspoon sea or kosher salt

1. In a skillet over medium heat, heat the oil. Add the ginger and chilies, and cook for 2 to 3 minutes.

2. Add the tomatoes and onions, and cook for 10 minutes.

3. In a blender, blend the tomato and onion mixture with the coconut, mustard seeds, urad dal, curry leaves, and salt until smooth.

4. If the consistency is too thick, add a touch of water until it reaches your desired thickness.

5. Serve.

Ayurvedic Lifestyle Tip: *Sleep is fundamental to health. Before bed, take a warm, soothing bath or drink a warm glass of organic milk, considered to be a sacred ingredient, 30 minutes before bed to help you fall asleep.*

GARLICKY TAHINI DRESSING WITH CUMIN

PREP TIME: 5 MINUTES

This perfect salad topper does wonders on a mezze platter as well. Check out the sides listed in this book, and serve a roundup along with this dressing and some chapati.

2 cups sesame oil

¼ cup nut or seed oil

1 cup freshly squeezed lemon juice

½ cup soy sauce

¾ cup tahini

5 garlic cloves

2 tablespoons mustard, mustard powder, or seeds

1 teaspoon sea or kosher salt

1 tablespoon ground cumin

¼ teaspoon cayenne powder

¾ cup water

1. In a blender, blend the sesame oil, nut oil, lemon juice, soy sauce, tahini, garlic, mustard, salt, cumin, cayenne, and water until smooth.

2. Adjust the consistency by adding more water or juice to thin or more tahini to thicken.

3. Serve atop a salad or as a dip with sides.

VATA

4
CUPS

SEASON: FALL

TASTES: ASTRINGENT, BITTER, PUNGENT, SALTY, SOUR, SWEET

Vatas *can add more heating spices, like paprika.*

Pittas *can use sunflower or coconut oils instead of the sesame and nut oils, lime juice instead of lemon, and tamari sauce instead of the soy sauce.*

Kaphas *can use sunflower, macadamia, or almond oils and use lime juice instead of lemon. Any additional herbs will work well, too.*

> **Mindfulness Tip:** *Scale down your day. Rather than overflowing your schedule with a mountain of tasks, prioritize. Concentrate on what needs to be done, and delegate or let go of what's not important. You'll remove stress and be more fully engaged in your priorities.*

SESAME GINGER DRESSING

PREP TIME: 5 MINUTES

PITTA

4

CUPS

SEASON: SUMMER

TASTES: ASTRINGENT, BITTER, PUNGENT, SALTY, SOUR, SWEET

Vatas can add more heating spices, like paprika and cayenne, and fresh garlic. Use lemon juice for the lime juice.

Pittas can use sunflower or coconut oils and omit the ginger.

Kaphas can use sunflower, macadamia, or almond oils. Any additional heating spices, like paprika or cayenne, will work well.

Sesame Ginger Dressing makes a great topping for tofu bowls, kitcharis, and almost any vegetable side dish featured in the book. Tamari, a substitute for soy sauce, is worth keeping on hand for pittas.

2 cups sesame oil

¼ cup olive oil

1 cup freshly squeezed lime juice

½ cup tamari sauce

3 garlic cloves

2 tablespoons turmeric

2 tablespoons ground ginger

1 teaspoon sea or kosher salt

1. In a blender, blend the sesame oil, olive oil, lime juice, tamari, garlic, turmeric, ginger, and salt until smooth.

2. Adjust the seasonings as desired and serve.

Ayurvedic Lifestyle Tip: *If you're a fan of pedicures, add a 10-minute foot massage to the treatment. It increases circulation and helps rid your body of excess weight. Or, if you've got a spouse or child up for the job, enroll them in helping you work out the kinks.*

LEMON YOGURT DRESSING

PREP TIME: 5 MINUTES

If you're looking for a dressing that does way more than top salads, this is it. Use it for side dishes, mezze platters, sandwiches, or wraps, or even as a smoothie base.

¾ cup Greek yogurt

6 tablespoons olive oil

3 tablespoons freshly squeezed lemon juice

Zest of 1 lemon

1 to 2 tablespoons tahini

1 tablespoon raw honey

1 tablespoon turmeric

½ tablespoon paprika

3 tablespoons water

Sea salt

Freshly ground black pepper

1. In a blender, blend the yogurt, oil, lemon juice, zest, tahini, honey, turmeric, paprika, and water until smooth.

2. Season with the salt and pepper and serve.

VATA

4–6
SERVINGS

SEASONS: FALL/WINTER

TASTES: ASTRINGENT, BITTER, PUNGENT, SALTY, SOUR, SWEET

Vatas *can add more heating spices, like paprika and cayenne, and fresh garlic.*

Pittas *can use coconut oil and freshly squeezed lime juice instead of olive oil and lemon juice. Add fresh basil or mint for cooling.*

Kaphas *can use soy yogurt and sunflower oil instead of the Greek yogurt and olive oil. In lieu of tahini, use almond butter.*

Timesaving Tip: *Dedicate one night a week (preferably a Sunday) to cooking as much as you can in large batches. Soups, stews, and vegetables or baked pastas can all be prepared days in advance. For instance, chicken breasts are ideal to bake in advance so they're ready for salad toppings, shredded tacos, or pastas when it's lunch or dinner time.*

SUN-DRIED TOMATO WALNUT BOLOGNESE

PREP TIME: 5 MINUTES / COOK TIME: 20 MINUTES

VATA

3
CUPS

SEASONS: FALL/WINTER

TASTES: ASTRINGENT, BITTER, PUNGENT, SALTY, SOUR, SWEET

Vatas can add more heating spices, like garlic, paprika, and cayenne, and fresh garlic.

Pittas can halve the chili and garlic and add spinach and fresh basil, parsley, or mint for cooling.

Kaphas can halve the tomatoes and add more heating spices and herbs, like cayenne and paprika, for more support.

This chunky, hearty faux Bolognese is vegetarian, but you won't know the difference thanks to thick, rich bites of sun-dried tomatoes and crunchy walnuts. The lemon zest brightens the dish.

3 tablespoons olive oil
1 onion, diced
5 garlic cloves, minced
¼ teaspoon red chili flakes
2 (14-ounce) jars sun-dried tomatoes in oil, drained
2 cups fresh Italian herbs, like basil, oregano, thyme, or sage
1 cup chopped toasted walnuts (instructions on page 142)
Zest of 1 lemon
Sea salt
Freshly ground black pepper

1. In a large skillet over medium heat, heat the oil and add the onion. Cook for 2 minutes.

2. Add the garlic and chili flakes, and cook for 5 to 8 minutes.

3. Add the sun-dried tomatoes, Italian herbs, and walnuts, and cook for another 10 minutes.

4. Garnish with the zest, salt, and pepper and serve.

Mindfulness Tip: *Dance! It sounds cliché to dance like no one's watching, but in fact, dancing to a song you love gets your heart racing, blood flowing, and energy up, while the beats keep you in tune to the music. There's no mind wandering when your favorite rhythms are pouring through your heart and soul.*

CREAMY AVOCADO PASTA SAUCE WITH LEMON ZEST

PREP TIME: 5 MINUTES

This sauce tastes as rich and indulgent as kaphas like, with a little spike of heat. Fantastic for pastas as well as a sauce for any pescaterians in your house, this versatile blend is sure to come in handy.

4 garlic cloves

2 tablespoons olive oil

3 tablespoons freshly squeezed lemon juice

¼ teaspoon red chili flakes

2 avocados, peeled and pitted

Zest of 1 lemon

¾ cup toasted pumpkin seeds or sunflower seeds (optional) (toasting instructions on pages 153 and 151)

Sea salt

Freshly ground black pepper

1. In a blender, blend the garlic, oil, lemon juice, chili, and avocados until smooth.

2. If the consistency is too thick, add 1 to 2 tablespoons of water to thin.

3. Garnish with the zest, seeds (if using), salt, and pepper and serve.

Ayurvedic Lifestyle Tip: *Keep a balanced weight. Being overweight or underweight can be equally detrimental to your body's long-term health and longevity. Exercise, a healthy diet, and smart lifestyle habits can help you regulate the number on your scale.*

KAPHA

2–4
SERVINGS

SEASON: SPRING

TASTES: ASTRINGENT, BITTER, PUNGENT, SALTY, SOUR, SWEET

Vatas *can add more sour tastes, like olives or a splash of vinegar, and serve on top of warm pasta to heat the sauce a touch.*

Pittas *can halve the chili and garlic and add spinach and fresh basil, parsley, or mint for cooling.*

Kaphas *can add more heating spices and herbs, like paprika or cayenne, for more support.*

VEGAN ALFREDO SAUCE WITH GARLIC AND HERBS

PREP TIME: 5 MINUTES / COOK TIME: 15 MINUTES

PITTA KAPHA

2
CUPS

SEASONS: WINTER/SPRING

TASTES: ASTRINGENT, BITTER, PUNGENT, SALTY, SWEET

Vatas *can also use ghee or hemp, seed, or nut oils instead of the olive oil as well as lemon juice or red chili flakes. Sage, thyme, oregano, and tarragon work well, too.*

Pittas *can use coconut oil instead of the olive oil. Saffron, mint, and dill work well, too.*

Kaphas *can use sunflower or almond oils instead of olive oil. Any additional herbs work well, especially those with heat.*

The secret to an amazing vegan Alfredo sauce is nut milk, preferably almond. Because grains are both sweet and sour, you'll get to enjoy all the flavors when you pour this sauce over pasta or rice.

¼ cup olive oil (or 1:1 olive oil and ghee)
2 garlic cloves, minced
¼ cup whole wheat flour
2½ cups almond milk
2 tablespoons chopped fresh basil
2 tablespoons chopped fresh parsley
2 tablespoons chopped fresh sage
¼ teaspoon ground nutmeg
Sea salt
Freshly ground black pepper

1. In a large skillet over medium heat, heat the olive oil and add the garlic. Cook for 2 minutes.

2. Stir in the flour, whisking until it's incorporated. Cook for 2 minutes.

3. Stir in the almond milk until smooth.

4. Bring the sauce to a boil, then lower the heat and add the basil, parsley, sage, and nutmeg.

5. Simmer the sauce for 5 minutes.

6. Season with the salt and pepper and serve.

HERBED ONION VEGETARIAN "GRAVY"

PREP TIME: 5 MINUTES / COOK TIME: 15 MINUTES

This faux gravy has all the heartiness and flavor of meat-based gravies but is suited for the vegetarian kapha. Vary the herbs depending on your taste preferences and dosha.

2 tablespoons plus ¼ cup ghee, divided

1 onion, diced

¼ cup barley flour

3 cups vegetable broth

2 tablespoons chopped fresh thyme

2 tablespoons chopped fresh sage

2 tablespoons chopped fresh tarragon

2 tablespoons chopped fresh parsley

Sea salt

Freshly ground black pepper

1. In a large saucepan over medium heat, melt 2 tablespoons of ghee and add the onion. Cook for 10 minutes.

2. Add the remaining ¼ cup of ghee, melt, and stir in the flour. Cook for 3 minutes.

3. Whisk in the vegetable broth, thyme, sage, tarragon, and parsley.

4. Season with the salt and pepper and serve.

KAPHA

3
CUPS

SEASON: SPRING

TASTES: ASTRINGENT, BITTER, PUNGENT, SALTY, SOUR, SWEET

Vatas *can add lemon, cayenne, and red chili flakes.*

Pittas *can add spinach and fresh mint.*

Kaphas *can add heating spices and herbs, like cayenne and paprika, for more support.*

Timesaving Tip: *Can you get it or do it online? Whether it's banking, grocery shopping, or gift buying, if you don't need to physically be at the store, bank, or boutique, complete the task online.*

CILANTRO–MINT MANGO SALSA

PREP TIME: 10 MINUTES

VATA   PITTA   KAPHA

2
CUPS

SEASONS: ALL SEASONS

TASTES: ASTRINGENT,
BITTER, PUNGENT,
SALTY, SWEET

Vatas *can add a splash of vinegar.*

Pittas *can halve the ginger and garlic.*

Kaphas *can use sunflower oil instead of olive oil and add more heating spices and herbs, like cayenne and paprika, for more support.*

Don't be fooled by the "salsa" in the name. This garnish-meets-dip can play in any meal or course, from breakfast eggs to lunch wraps to Asian dinner takeout. It's as creative as your menu.

1 cup minced fresh cilantro
1 cup minced fresh mint
6 garlic cloves, minced
1 mango, peeled, pitted, and chopped
¼ to ½ cup minced fresh ginger
½ to ¾ cup olive oil
Sea salt
Freshly ground black pepper

1. In a medium bowl, whisk the cilantro, mint, garlic, mango, ginger, and olive oil.

2. Season with the salt and pepper and serve.

Mindfulness Tip: *Walk in the woods. The Japanese practice of forest bathing, called shinrin yoku, literally means "bathing your senses in the forest." Spend 15 minutes a day walking outdoors or in nature, and notice the birds chirping, the leaves rustling, the river trickling by. Doing so reduces stress, boosts immunity, and helps your mind practice observing what's around you.*

ALMOND–CILANTRO PESTO

PREP TIME: 5 MINUTES

Make a batch of this on a Sunday night, and use it all week to top tofu bowls, stir-fries, pastas, sandwiches, and proteins. It also makes a great dip for crackers.

¾ cup toasted almonds (follow walnut-toasting instructions on
    page 142)
2 cups packed fresh cilantro leaves
3 garlic cloves
1 cup olive oil
Juice of 1 lime
1 teaspoon red chili flakes
Sea salt
Freshly ground black pepper

1. In a blender, pulse the almonds, cilantro, garlic, olive oil, lime juice, and red chili flakes until smooth. If too thick, add water (use reserved pasta water if you're making pasta with this pesto).

2. Season with the salt and pepper and serve.

KAPHA

2

CUPS

SEASON: SPRING

TASTES: ASTRINGENT, BITTER, PUNGENT, SALTY, SOUR, SWEET

Vatas *can add more heating spices, like paprika and cayenne, and lemon juice.*

Pittas *can use coconut oil in place of olive oil and add fresh basil or mint for cooling.*

Kaphas *can use pumpkin or sunflower seeds with or instead of the almonds.*

Ayurvedic Lifestyle Tip: *Ensure a peaceful night's sleep by avoiding negative thoughts, worry, or stress before bed. One hour before bed, turn off electronics, like computers and TVs, and avoid reading the news or exercising before falling asleep.*

GLOSSARY

DOSHA: One of three energies—kapha, pitta and vata—that make up your physical, mental, and spiritual constitution.

GUNA: Ayurveda breaks up food, medicine, and people into three "gunas"—tamasic, sattvic, or rajasic—that describe their dominant nature, characteristics, and unique qualities. Gunas are sometimes referred to as mind doshas.

HALWA: A traditional Indian sweet dessert made of carrots boiled with milk and spices.

HOLISM: In medicine, this refers to the idea of treating, or examining, the whole person, including lifestyle habits, exercise routines, and diet, rather than a symptom or illness.

KAPHA DOSHA: The energetic constitution that represents the elements of earth and water and is largely associated with stability, relaxation, and peace.

KITCHARI: Tridoshic dishes made from beans and rice used to aid digestion and detoxify or cleanse your body of toxins.

PITTA DOSHA: The energetic constitution that represents the elements of earth and fire and is largely associated with metabolism, energy, and transformation.

RAITA: An Indian condiment made from yogurt, spices, and vegetables typically used to cool spicy foods.

RAJASIC: One of the three mind doshas. Rajasic deals with anger, greed, sensuality, and jealousy and relates to foods that are sour, salty, pungent, hot, dry, or bitter.

SATTVIC: One of the three mind doshas. Sattvic deals with balance and energy and relates to foods that are nourishing, juicy, light, and fresh.

SYNERGISM: This refers to the cooperation of two or more substances. For example, Ayurveda working synergistically with you and your lifestyle means that it interacts with and works in combination with your life, versus changing or overhauling it.

TAMASIC: One of the three mind doshas. Tamasic deals with doubt, ignorance, laziness, negativity, worry, and fear and relates to foods that are spoiled, unpalatable, dry, expired, or unhealthy.

TRIDOSHIC: Balancing all dosha types.

VATA DOSHA: The energetic constitution that represents the elements of air and space and is largely associated with mobility and the nervous system.

RESOURCES

Enjoy these other books and sites for additional information about Ayurveda.

Books

Ayurveda: The Science of Self Healing (Lotus Press, 1985) by Vasant Lad

Eat, Taste, Heal: An Ayurvedic Cookbook for Modern Living (Five Elements Press, 2006) by Thomas Yarema, Daniel Rhoda, Johnny Brannigan

Prakriti: Your Ayurvedic Constitution (Lotus Press, 1998) by Dr. Robert Svoboda

The Ayurveda Bible (Firefly Books, 2012) by Anne McIntyre

Websites

Ayurveda Dosha,
http://ayurvedadosha.org

Banyan Botanicals,
www.banyanbotanicals.com

Dosha Guru,
http://doshaguru.com

Everyday Ayurveda,
www.everydayayurveda.org

Food for Awakening,
www.foodforawakening.com

Food Pyramid,
www.foodpyramid.com

Holistic Online,
http://holisticonline.com

Joyful Belly,
www.joyfulbelly.com

Mind, Body, Green,
www.mindbodygreen.com

Mudita Institute,
http://muditainstitute.com

Nature's Formulary,
http://naturesformulary.com

Peace Tree Healing,
www.peacetreehealing.com

San Diego College of Ayurveda,
http://sandiegocollegeofayurveda.net

The Chopra Center,
www.chopra.com

The Natural Epicurean,
http://naturalepicurean.com

APPENDIX: CONVERSION CHARTS

VOLUME EQUIVALENTS (LIQUID)

US STANDARD	US STANDARD (OUNCES)	METRIC (APPROXIMATE)
2 tablespoons	1 fl. oz.	30 mL
¼ cup	2 fl. oz.	60 mL
½ cup	4 fl. oz.	120 mL
1 cup	8 fl. oz.	240 mL
1½ cups	12 fl. oz.	355 mL
2 cups or 1 pint	16 fl. oz.	475 mL
4 cups or 1 quart	32 fl. oz.	1 L
1 gallon	128 fl. oz.	4 L

OVEN TEMPERATURES

FAHRENHEIT (F)	CELSIUS (C) (APPROXIMATE)
250	120
300	150
325	165
350	180
375	190
400	200
425	220
450	230

VOLUME EQUIVALENTS (DRY)

US STANDARD	METRIC (APPROXIMATE)
⅛ teaspoon	0.5 mL
¼ teaspoon	1 mL
½ teaspoon	2 mL
¾ teaspoon	4 mL
1 teaspoon	5 mL
1 tablespoon	15 mL
¼ cup	59 mL
⅓ cup	79 mL
½ cup	118 mL
⅔ cup	156 mL
¾ cup	177 mL
1 cup	235 mL
2 cups or 1 pint	475 mL
3 cups	700 mL
4 cups or 1 quart	1 L
½ gallon	2 L
1 gallon	4 L

WEIGHT EQUIVALENTS

US STANDARD	METRIC (APPROXIMATE)
½ ounce	15 g
1 ounce	30 g
2 ounces	60 g
4 ounces	115 g
8 ounces	225 g
12 ounces	340 g
16 ounces or 1 pound	455 g

INDEX

DOSHA INDEX

VATA

CPSIA information can be obtained
at www.ICGtesting.com
Printed in the USA
LVOW05s2005030617

536717LV00005B/6/P